MW01244490

# Transformed in His Presence

## A Journey of Healing through Christ

By

### April Farris

Transformed in His Presence
© 2020 by April Farris

All rights reserved. No portion of this book may be copied, transmitted, or used in any form without prior written permission.

Unless otherwise noted all scripture quotations are from *The Holy Bible*, English Standard Version® Copyright © 2001 by Crossway Bibles, a publishing ministry of Good News Publishers. Used by permission. All rights reserved.

The following Bible translations were used:

*The Amplified® Bible (AMP)*
Copyright © 2015 by The Lockman Foundation
Used by permission. www.Lockman.org

*The Amplified® Bible (AMPC)*
Copyright © 1954, 1958, 1962, 1964, 1965, 1987 by The Lockman Foundation
Used by permission. www.Lockman.org

Contemporary English Version
Copyright © 1991, 1992, 1995 by American Bible Society, Used by permission.

*The Message,*
Copyright © 1993, 1994, 1995, 1996, 2000, 2001, 2002. Used by permission of NavPress Publishing Group.

The New King James Version,
Copyright © 1982 by Thomas Nelson, Inc. Used by permission. All rights reserved.

Dedication:
This book is dedicated to the Lord Jesus Christ who bore my pain
on the cross so that I could be healed.

## Thank you:

- to my husband, Mike for his dedication and love for me and this project. You have loved me as I have walked through my healing and supported this book from its beginning.

- to my daughters, Nicole, Erica and Bethann celebrating God's goodness in His healing of me and applying His grace to me in the healing process.

- to the midwive intercessors who helped give birth to this book: Cindy M., Dorene B., and the dynamic Traci M. and Tracie M. duo. You were all my biggest cheerleaders.

- to Nicole Raimo for the final editing of this book that brings it to completion. It was your prayers that pulled the words from God's throne room to my heart, and from my heart to these pages!

- to the first two Healing Presence groups which allowed me to impart the words on these pages in person to them.

Lastly to our church, LivingStones Communities: thank you for loving me and supporting me in this process.

# Transformed in His Presence

## A Journey of Healing through Christ

# Contents

*Foreword*........................................................................ 13

Introduction................................................................... 14

**Pre-journey Preparation** ........................................ **19**

**Section I – The Upward Journey Journey to the Heart of God**
.............................................................................. **25**

Chapter 1- Practicing His Presence............................... 35

Chapter 2 - Meditating on His Glory ............................ 55

Chapter 3 - Journaling His Love.................................... 75

**Section II – The Inward Journey Journey into the Depths of**
**our Hearts**................................................................. **99**

Chapter 4- Opening Our Hearts ................................... 105

Chapter 5 - His Healing Presence ............................... 129

Chapter 6 - Run to the Cross....................................... 153

Chapter 7- A New Heart .............................................. 177

**Section III – The Outward Journey, Sharing the Journey**
**with Others**.............................................................. **207**

Chapter 8 - Created to BE............................................ 211

Chapter 9 - Manifesting His Glory .............................. 237

Chapter 10 - Manifesting His Presence ...................... 261

More of God's Attributes: ........................................................ 285

His Healing Love ..................................................................... 287

In Christ .................................................................................. 291

Contact the author                                293

End Notes                                           295

# Foreword

I met April Farris, and her husband Mike, over ten years ago when we served together with several churches in a discipleship program in Cleveland Ohio. One of my first impressions of April was that she was a Jesus lover. There are some Christians who don't seem to have a personal relationship with the Lord. For them, reading the Bible, praying daily, attending church, and other activities associated with Christianity are viewed as necessary steps to reach their goal to live a good life so they can go to heaven when they die. However, every now and then I meet people who are passionately in love with Jesus. Their lives are built around persuing and living in the presence of God. April is one of those people. It is hard to have a conversation with her about God without recognizing her sensitivity to Holy Spirit and her brokenness in His presence.

April is a student of the Word. She completed Old and New Testament surveys through Moody Bible Institute and attended the College of Prayer in Vermillion, Ohio. She was ordained as a minister of the Gospel under Cindy Jacob's Reformation Prayer Network. She is commissioned by Greg and Rebecca Greenwood as an Apostolic Coordinator for the Strategic Prayer Apostolic Network and is presently in training with Rebecca in the school of Prophesy and Strategic level Spiritual Warfare. She has also attended Prophetic Clinic Seminars which I have taught. April has traveled nationally and Internationally with the Pastoral Care School team ministering Healing and Deliverance. She is a student of Wagner University working towards her Doctorate of Apostolic Leadership and Theology.

April serves alongside her husband, Mike Farris, as they lead an Apostolic Center, *LivingStones Communities,* in Cleveland, Ohio. She also serves in team with several organizations in the greater Cleveland area. She has helped and ministered to hundreds of people through seminars in the areas of prayer and intercession, principles of the prophetic,and healing the sick and deliverance. Her participation in these assignments has taken her to various cities in the U.S.A. and nations of the world.

Considering all of the above and much more, I am excited to write this foreword for April. In my forty plus years of ministry, I am still inspired and encouraged to see leaders walking in their God given assignment.

In this book, *Transformed in His Presence,* April shares how her Christian life had become mundane and monotonous. She was going through the rituals of being a believer, but she was not seeing any results. She was very discontent and spiritually hungry, which set her on a journey to discover more about God. As a result, she began to experience the fulfillment of the Father's promise that "You will seek me and find me, when you search for me with all your heart." (Jeremiah 29:13 NASB)

This book is more than a typical devotional. April's approach is personal and practical yet engaging. She shares the importance of knowing God through His word, knowing God through His healing presence and knowing God through His character. She helps you dig into the scriptures by asking thought-provoking questions to draw you deeper into understanding God not only as Lord and King but also as Father. This book will help you get more out of your Bible study, be more consistent in prayer, and most of all to be *Transformed in His Presence.*

Gary Pleasant, Apostolic leader, Kingdom Ministries International

## *Introduction*

I became a Christian in 1985, and for the most part I was content in my relationship with the Lord. However, as the years went by, I felt constantly defeated in my walk and felt an inner struggle. I served in a lot of ministries; in fact, I kept myself very busy thinking I was "doing God's work." But my life seemed to function more out of religious duty than out of a relationship with the Living God. My lifestyle was one of negativity and emptiness instead of joy and contentment. I constantly seemed to struggle through devotions that always seemed dry, and I found myself asking, "Is there more to this life with Christ than I'm living?"

I began asking the Lord why I had so many health problems and why it seemed that I could not overcome certain areas of sin in my life. Over time I discovered I did not like who I was, and my life did not seem to show any Fruit of the Spirit. I came to realize that "doing God's work" was missing something: Him. This started me on a journey to discover more about the God I claimed to serve. God used my questioning and emptiness to start me on a journey of discovering who He is, discovering who I am, and ultimately discovering who He wants me to become.

This journey began by learning to look upward to Him. It was about discovering who the Father, Son and Holy Spirit were and how we were to relate to each other. The more I sought to know Him, the more my relationship began to change from one of religious study to one of intimacy with my God. It was no longer a duty but an excitement! I could not wait to come to the Father, spend time with Him, discover a new aspect of Him, and apply that to my life. From this relationship, my heart changed, and I felt a deeper intimacy with the Lord unlike any I had ever experienced.

The Lord promises in Jeremiah 29:13, "Then you will seek Me, inquire for, *and* require Me [as a vital necessity] and find Me when you search for Me with all your heart." (AMPC) That is what kept me pursuing the Father; a whole heart desire to meet Him as Moses did, face to face. The more I hungered to know who He was, the more He would reveal Himself. He became the lover of my soul, my "All in All." I was so open and hungry that whatever He asked for I wanted to give to Him. And He did ask.

Eventually, God told me that there was more to this journey He wanted to take me to a place that would deepen our relationship beyond what I could ever imagine. He said that this part of the journey would be difficult. He wanted intimacy with me as much as I wanted it with Him. He showed me that Intimacy really means "In-To-Me-He-Sees." This journey inward was to reveal the true condition of my heart. He showed me that the many years of pain I had experienced were keeping me from being closer to Him. He likened this journey to a woman giving birth: her pain was temporary but the joy of the reward that followed afterward was inexpressible. In His gentle way, as only the Lord can, He was giving me a choice. He promised He would never give me anything I couldn't bear, promised He would never leave me or forsake me, and promised that He would be by my side every step of the way.

So together, hand in hand, we started our journey inward to the depths of my heart. Along this journey we would come to barriers that He would reveal as diseased parts of my heart.

He would ask for this part of my heart and I would surrender it to him. When He was finished, a heart surgery had taken place; He had replaced my stony cold heart with a new soft heart.

After a period of healing, He began showing me how to use this new heart and how to protect it from becoming like the old one. He asked if I was ready for a new journey – the outward journey – to come out of myself and live a new transformed life that was visible to others.

God explained to me that the outward journey was to show His manifested presence to the world. Just as He said to His Son Jesus, He said to me, "This is my daughter in whom I am well pleased." He had given me a new heart and had put a new spirit within me. It was time to test it. It was time to use my new heart for His glory, that all may see His reflection in my life. It was at this time that the fruit of the Spirit began to overflow like streams of living water, showering everyone who came near with blessings from the Father. It was also a time of a greater manifestation of His Spirit.

I find that one no sooner begins to feel comfortable with the outward journey than God seems to start placing a new hunger within, and the journey changes and starts over again in a new direction.

The journey for each of us is a never-ending circle of His love allowing us to draw ever closer to Him. Each time God changes the direction of our journey, it seems to go deeper into the heart of the Father. He continually grants a deeper healing within our hearts. We then experience a greater outpouring of Him upon us that we may better impact the world with His Glory and His Healing Presence. As you travel on your journey, it is my prayer that you will experience a greater measure of the Lord and that He will manifest His glory in you and through you.

A journey is more fun to take with others, so it may be helpful to ask a friend to take this journey with you. However, if you chose to study this on your own, know that the Lord will be with you. As with any journey, there are some necessities you will need to take with you. The most important, of course, is your Bible. You will need several pens to write down in this book all the exciting things you learn along the way. I would also suggest that you have several selections of worship music readily available. Your local Christian bookstore can be a great resource for this if you do not already have some praise and worship music on hand. The only other thing you need to bring with you is your desire and hunger to be with the Lord.

You will want to leave all other baggage behind. However, if you should choose to bring it anyway, please understand that eventually you will be asked to give it up along the way. So relax, and let's get started on our "journey to the heart of God."

# Pre-journey Preparation

Before you can begin the upward journey into the heart of God you must first see if you meet the prerequisites for the journey. Romans 3:23 says, "For all have sinned and fall short of the glory of God." In other words, none of us are worthy to take this journey because of our sin. So how can we journey to the heart of God? We must first have permission to travel. We need a passport. John 14:6 says, "Jesus said to him, I am the Way and the Truth and the Life; no one comes to the Father except by (through) Me." (AMPC) We need to ask his Son, Jesus, for permission. An exchange must occur. We must be willing to agree with Romans 3:23 and John 14:6. If we agree with this, then the promise is found in Romans 6:23 which states, "For the wages of sin is death, but the free gift of God is eternal life in Christ Jesus our Lord."

If you have not confessed that you are a sinner, repented of your sins, and received God's Son as Lord over your whole life, you cannot have access to the Father's heart. If you have already confessed your sins and have received Jesus Christ as Lord and Savior of your life, then your passport is in order, and you are ready for the journey.

If you are not sure, or if you have never prayed to receive Christ, then please pray the prayer shown below right now. Pray this prayer aloud.

*Dear God,*

*I recognize that I am a sinner. I have sinned in many ways, including making other things gods in my life. I realize that I have been in control of my life, and today I want to make You*

*Lord over every area of my life. I choose to turn away from my old lifestyle, thoughts, and habits and give them to You to transform and make new. Please forgive me for my sins. I ask You to rule in every part of my life. Today I choose to submit my life to the only true, living God. I thank You for sending me Your Son, the Lord Jesus, as a sacrifice for my sins. Please fill me with Your Holy Spirit so I can live with every area of my life surrendered to You daily. In Jesus' name, Amen.*

If you have prayed this prayer, sign your name and the date of this decision. Please contact our ministry as well to let us know about your decision. We want to celebrate with you and welcome you into the family of God!

Name: _____ Date _____

Now you have your passport! You are ready to take the journey. As you begin the journey, here are some roadblocks to avoid:

### Roadblock #1 – Missing your daily time with the Lord.

To remain consistent in your journey and to prevent burnout, you must make every effort to commit to a daily time with the Lord. Psalm 1:2 says, "But his delight *and* desire are in the law of the Lord, and on His law (the precepts, the instructions, the teachings of God) he habitually meditates (ponders and studies) by day and by night." (AMPC) If you miss a day though, don't try to get caught up, as this only adds pressure and feelings of frustration. Look at each day as a new journey with the Lord. These lessons are meant to be put into practice daily, but they are also small, bite-sized pieces so you can start with 10 - 15 minutes a day and build from there. It's not the quantity of the time you spend with the Lord but the quality. Quantity flows naturally from quality!

### *Roadblock #2 – The trap of "busyness" and the struggle to be still.*

With all the noise in our world, it is often difficult to hear the Lord's voice. We in America have become so used to having noise around us constantly that we've forgotten the discipline of sitting in silence. Many scriptures refer to being still, listening, and waiting on the Lord. Living in a society where we are so media-focused causes us to be uncomfortable with silence. Psalm 37:7a says, *"Be still before the Lord; wait patiently for Him and entrust yourself to Him;"* (AMP)

### *Roadblock #3 – Finding a place to spend time with the Lord.*

I know of people who are unable to find a designated place to comfortably spend time with the Lord. What settled it for me was when I read Psalm 149:5, which says, *"Let the saints be joyful in the glory and beauty [which God confers upon them]; let them sing for joy upon their beds."* (AMPC) My Bible, journal, CD player and all my music CD's are on my nightstand.

The key is to find a place that suits you and that you make a choice and then stick with it. Once you find a place, pray and ask the Lord to bless that place as your altar. Dedicate it to Him in prayer as a place you and He will meet daily. Even when I am traveling, I find a place and dedicate it to the Lord.

21

If at any time you hit one of these roadblocks, know that Jesus is always there to help you overcome it. Don't become discouraged - just begin each day as if it is a new journey with Him.

Let's start this journey together with a prayer:

*Dear Father God,*

*I dedicate my time and schedule to you. I pray that You will help me overcome each roadblock that may come my way. In Jesus' name, Amen.*

Write what you expect in this journey with God and what you are hoping to experience. Feel free to even write your fears.

_____

_____

_____

_____

_____

_____

_____

_____

_____

_____

_____

# Section I – The Upward Journey

# Journey to the Heart of God

# The Journey Begins

In the upward Journey section of this book you will begin to draw closer to the Lord by learning to communicate and bond with your Heavenly Father through worship and prayer. Here we begin to abandon "self", to learn and develop a whole heart devotion to the Lord. We won't have just a casual relationship with The Bible, the book that represents God; His words will become a living, breathing instrument. His words will become a living, breathing instrument that will draw us into a place of intimacy with Him. We will learn how to live and walk in the presence of the Lord every moment of the day rather than giving Him just a few minutes of our time.

Let's face it: it's hard fitting everything we want to do into the hours we have. Now that we have given our lives over to the Lord, our schedules need to be yielded up to Him. You will find that it is in everyday living that it becomes hard to maintain a focus on the Lord. When a trial or difficulty hits, it is even harder to stay focused on the Lord. In our upward journey we will learn to look beyond our circumstances as Hebrews 12:2 states, "Looking away [from all that will distract] to Jesus, Who is the Leader *and* the Source of our faith." (AMPC)

God wooed us to Himself through His love and saved us. The enemy will do anything to distract, cause doubt, and cause us to stop focusing on Him. Jeremiah 29:13 states, "And you will seek Me and find *Me* when you search for Me <u>with your whole heart.</u>" (NKJV) [emphasis added] The upward journey is the pursuit of the Lover of our soul. It is in this place that we learn to abide (stay and rest quietly), so that when the storms of life come at us, we learn to see them from His perspective. Learning to practice His presence we learn to sit with Him in the heavenly places, seeing things as He sees them. We must always maintain a desire and deep yearning for Him at all times. This will help us to push through all the distractions that come at us.

Have you ever been at a picnic and just as you sit down to eat, flies appear and start landing on your food? You either have to press through and keep eating, choosing to not let them bother you, or you pack it all up and bring the food inside to eat. Distractions are like flies - you either choose to let them ruin your whole day or you press on and choose to enjoy them. When we are faithful, His love and peace will flood our hearts and minds and consume us.

When we finally reach that place of being in His presence, we don't want to leave. We lay our heads on His breast and listen as His heart beats. With every beat, words and expressions of His love flow out to us. You may find this difficult at first and that is okay. It has taken many years to become the person you are; changes will not happen overnight. Just be faithful to Him, and He promises He will be faithful to you.

Like a young child learning to communicate with his parents, you will learn to communicate with your Heavenly Father. And how do we do this? We communicate with God through prayer. Don't let this word intimidate you! Prayer is simply speaking to God and expressing your thoughts.

When the disciples asked Jesus how they were to pray, He gave them this example: "Our Father in heaven, hallowed be your name. Your kingdom come, Your will be done on earth

28

as *it is* in heaven." (Luke 11:2) (NKJV) Jesus told his disciples in this example to begin by acknowledging the Father's presence with praise (words of adoration)

The Bible says that when we praise God this:

• Evokes the presence of God (Psalm 22:3)

• Defeats the enemy (2 Chronicles 20: 20-22)

• Changes the way we see our circumstances (Hebrews 12:2)

• Builds up our faith (Jude 1:20)

During this journey, you will be asked to use your imagination to see the scriptures come alive in a new way. As adults, we think that using our imagination is child-like, so we don't often use this part of our mind. Instead, we fill our minds with outside influences through various forms of the media – television, movies, magazines, etc. Using our imagination to meditate on scripture helps purify our mind and counteracts those outside influences.

Scripture tells us in Philippians 4:8, "Finally, brethren, whatever things are true, whatever things are noble, whatever things are just, whatever things are pure, whatever things are lovely, whatever things are of good report, if there is any virtue and if there is anything praiseworthy—meditate on these things." (NKJV) [emphasis added]

If you find using your imagination difficult at any time, just place your hand on your head and ask the Lord to bring healing to your imagination. This difficulty (often) occurs because of things you have looked at in the past that were ungodly.

Once, I went on a fast from TV to cleanse my mind. You see, our eyes and ears are gateways to our souls (our mind, will and emotions); when we watch or look upon ungodly things, we are opening our souls to impure things. This is why we feel fearful when we watch a movie that is frightening, which can also then affect our dreams; we may have nightmares and be tormented when we try to sleep. By praying over our minds and repenting of every impure thought that surfaces, we will begin to have a pure mind (Matthew 6:22-23). As you do this, not only will you begin to use your imagination in a better way, but your soul will also be able to discern and learn to hear the voice of the Lord better as well. All your senses will begin to become heightened, and you will be able to better sense His presence with you, in you, behind you, and before you. You will begin to experience His love in many new ways as you put into practice the things in each lesson.

During this journey, we will also begin to journal. This is a great way for you to express yourself. If you're not used to journaling, stick with it and you will find your journal becomes a great way to keep track of your experiences along the way. How awesome to have these memories of your journey together with the Lord! You never know when He may whisper a scripture, give you a song, or show you a picture. Write these down for they are special – just for you. Your journal records the conversations you have with the Lord and this will build your faith.

A few years ago, when I was struggling with hearing the Lord, I wrote these words to Him in my journal. (It was from my heart to the Lord's heart, and He responded back to me!)

## I will wait for You

*Lord, I will wait for You, as long as it takes to hear Your voice.*
*I will wait for You, for what You have to say to me, I want to hear.*
*I will wait for You, just so I can hear You speak one more time.*

*There are so many noises in the world,*
*I can't seem to hear You when You speak.*
*I keep searching to find that place of solace*
*but it's been so difficult for me.*

*Then there are other days when I am being pulled both to the right and to the left.*
*I can hear Your Spirit calling, "But I don't have time," I said.*
*Then I heard Him say...*
*"I will wait for you as long as it takes just to hear your voice.*
*I will wait for you,*
*for what you have to say, I want to hear.*
*I will wait for you just so I can hear you say 'I love you.'"*

The Lord is waiting for you now with open arms! He wants to welcome you into this time with Him. He knows the road it took to get you here.

**The different parts of each lesson**

The overall goal is for us to spend time in both His Word and in His Presence. Each lesson includes four sections. You can choose to either do one lesson a day or break it down to one lesson a week. Work at your own pace.

For this journey you will need a road map: the Bible. The first section of each lesson is called "Our Daily Bread" where we read and study the Bible together. The Bible is His written Word to us and is literally our daily manna (bread). Just like the manna of the Old Testament, it grows stale if you try to save it for the next day; God wants you to eat fresh manna from Him, daily. The more we hear His voice, the more we will hunger to meet Him daily. When we study scriptures, you will see that the Bible is filled with stories about regular people like you and me. This section includes a few questions to help you dig deep in your understanding of His Word.

The second section is called "Journey to the Father's heart." Here, you will practice being in His healing presence. This section gives you time to interact with the Lord as you "chew on his manna."

The third section is called "Bonding with the Father". These are scriptures that will help you further study His character and get to know Him better. These are great to study either during your quiet time or periodically throughout the day.

The last section of each lesson is a scripture verse for you to memorize. Scripture says in Psalm 119:11, *"Your word I have hidden in my heart that I might not sin against you."* It is important to store God's Word in your heart so that you have a fluid resource to draw upon in time of need. Memorizing the Word becomes a vital weapon when spoken out of the mouth of a child of God!

You will also see that I have included pages on which you can journal while you spend time with the Lord. As I mentioned before, this is to help you remember what the Lord has spoken and done for you. This will be your own book of remembrance. Journaling is a very important discipline in getting to know God better in this journey. Please make every effort to be faithful in writing down your thoughts and experiences. Your obedience in this will bring you greater revelation and insight into the very heart of God.

Allow me to pray for you as you start your new journey:

*Dear Precious Heavenly Father,*

*I pray for Your precious ones as they begin this exciting journey with You - that You will take them to new levels of intimacy with You. I pray for a deeper hunger and yearning that can only be met by You. I pray they will not give up until You have met them in a fresh way. Give them this day their daily bread (manna). I pray especially that they will be able to keep their eyes focused on You and will learn to see the circumstances in their life as You do. Bless them, Lord, to daily move closer to You. In Jesus' name. Amen.*

# Chapter 1

# Practicing His Presence

# Lesson 1 - Touching the Father's heart

*"I will meditate on your majestic, glorious splendor and*
*your wonderful works"*
*Psalm 145:5 (NKJV)*

Of all the people of the Bible, David was the one who could touch the heart of the heavenly Father through his words and songs of praise and worship. *Vines Concise Dictionary* defines worship in the Old Testament as "to prostrate oneself, bow down, to come before God and worship". The most frequently used word for worship in the New Testament is *proskuneo*, which means, "to kiss."[1] Please note that there is a distinct difference between Old Testament worship and New Testament worship. Jesus' death on the cross removed the veil of separation between God and His people, allowing us direct access to our Heavenly Father. In the Old Testament, people worshipped at a distance; in the New Testament, we can worship intimately with him, close enough to give Him a loving kiss.

Offering up praise and worship to God is not something that comes naturally to us as Christians. However, it is the very thing that can draw us closer to Him. As we learn to come before the Lord with praise and worship, we begin to learn more about who He is and more about His character. When we begin to worship Him in spirit and in truth (John 4:24), we exchange our gloomy human state of being for the glorious reality of Jesus Christ.

The Father loves to hear His children tell Him how much we love Him. Lifting praise to our Abba is telling Him how much we adore Him. It is blessing His character; it is exalting His name over all other names in heaven or on earth; it is simply telling Him how much we love Him and need Him. This is not to be a duty that we simply perform. It is to be an act of love. As with any love relationship, it starts by acknowledging His love for us and speaking out our love to Him. If we truly love the Lord with all our heart, with all our soul, and with our entire mind and all our strength, then we should want to worship Him in spirit and in truth (Mark 12:30; John 4:24). Adoring the Father through songs, hymns, and spiritual songs should be an outward expression of the love we feel for Him. It won't be easy, but with practice and prayer the Lord will grant a heart of worship. All we need to do is ask.

So, let's begin this upward journey together to the Father's heart!

### David, a man after God's heart (1 Samuel 16:14-23)

David lived a lifestyle of praise and worship to the Lord. As a young shepherd boy, he would sit out in the fields playing and singing to the Lord. Worshipping God seemed to be a natural expression of his love for the Lord. Even as he would sit out under the stars in the cold, lonely night, he was able to praise God for His creation (Psalm 19). As he grew older, God used his music to soothe King Saul's restless heart and mind.

**Read Psalm 19 & 1 Samuel 16:14-23.  Then answer the following:**

1.  Write some words of praise you find in these passages

_____

_____

_____

_____

2.  What kind of instrument did David play? _____

3.  Who suggested the idea of music to Saul? _____

4.  What kind of spirit was said to be bothering Saul?

_____

5.  What do you think was different about David's music versus that of any other musician who could have played in Saul's court? (Read 1 Samuel 16:13)

_____

_____

6.  What effect did David's music have upon Saul's mood and mind?

_____

_____

7. What effect did David's music have on the spirit affecting Saul?

_____

_____

### *Journey to the Father's Heart*

When you are distressed, what do you do? How does this benefit you? What should you do when you are feeling distressed? (Write your thoughts in your journal found at the end of this section.)

As you read and meditate on these scriptures above, think about what kind of heart we should bring to the Lord. (Write your thoughts in your journal or on the following pages.)

Let's spend some time together in His healing presence: (pray in your own words)

*Dear Lord,*

*Forgive me for the times I have felt worried or anxious. I know that this is considered a sin to you. Help me to remember to come to you **first** when I begin to feel distressed, worried, or anxious. Help me to learn to praise you with a true heart of worship. Help me to learn to express my love to you. Give me the words to what I feel in my heart. Amen.*

Spend time with the Lord this week by entering His presence through worship. Express love and a longing to be with Him! Feel free to use any worship music that appeals to you.

During this time, do not ask anything of Him – just worship Him.

**Journaling:**

In the following lines keep track of your spiritual journey into His presence. Write down anything you experience while you spend time with Him in worship.

Include any difficulties that you are experiencing, either in worshipping the Lord or in your life. Then turn these struggles into words of thanksgiving to Him. Example: "Lord, I thank You that in the midst of this struggle {name the struggle}, You are in control." Then listen for a response from Him. Remember! This requires you to be still and know that He is God (Psalm 46:10).

_____

_____

_____

_____

_____

_____

_____

_____

_____

_____

_____

_____

_____

_____

_____

_____

_____

_____

_____

_____

_____

_____

Bonding with your Heavenly Father is an important part of worshipping Him. This is how you come to better understand His character and get to know Him and His marvelous attributes. Read these scriptures slowly, and meditate on who God is in your life.

**Bonding with the Father**
❖ **Psalm 105:1-10**
❖ **Psalm 138**
❖ **Psalm 145**
❖ **Psalm 29**

**Memorize:**

*"Enter His gates with thanksgiving; go into His courts with praise. Give thanks to Him and bless His name." Psalm 100:4*

# Lesson 2 - Intimacy with Christ

*"You will seek me and find me; when you seek me with all your heart..."*
*Jeremiah 29:13*

When my children were toddlers, we used to play a word game. I would say, "I love you." They would answer back, "I love you, too." I would respond with "I love you three." They would say, "I love you four." We would go on like this depending on how high they had learned to count. The older they became, the higher the numbers reached. Eventually they got quicker, and their responses would be "I love you 15, 16, 17, 18, 19, 20." They would even start counting by fives and then tens. We would have fun racing and shouting over each other to see who could get to the highest number the quickest. Often, I would just let them win. They would be so excited because they were learning to count and expressing their love at the same time.

One day as we were playing this game, my sister-in-law said that she and her son played the same game. But while they were playing, instead of racing to get to the highest number the fastest, he said to her, "I love you infinity." She was surprised by his answer, not realizing that he even knew what the word meant. She decided to ask him what he felt that meant and he opened wide his arms and said, "It's this much, mommy." When I heard her tell the story, I immediately thought of Christ and how He showed His love to us by opening wide His arms to be nailed on the cross. Our relationship with our children reminded me of how we need

43

to come to Christ like our children come to us, with a heart of adoration to be able to express words or songs of love. Sometimes an expression of love is not even through words but simply through sitting still, holding each other, and feeling that security of being safe in the arms of the one you love and who loves you.

**John, the disciple Jesus loved (John 21:20)**

John, the disciple, knew what it was like to express love to Christ and to receive love from Him, much the same way a child receives love from a loving parent. John was the son of Zebedee and the brother of James. He and James were given the nickname "Sons of Thunder" by Jesus, possibly stemming from the time they asked Jesus to order fire down from heaven (Mark 3:17; Luke 9:54). John knew Christ in an intimate way because he had experienced the strong and personal love of the Son of God day in and day out for several years. The night of the Last Supper was one of those intimate times with Jesus. It was out of this love relationship that John wrote the Gospel of John, 1st, 2nd, 3rd John, as well as Revelation.

**Read Luke 9:46-56; John 13:21-25; Mark 9:2-10; John 19: 25-27; Acts 4:13**

1. What was John's reaction when Jesus was not able to go into the Samaritan Village?

_____

_____

2. What is John's character like in these passages?

_____

_____

3. What was Jesus' response to John in Luke 9:50?

_____

_____

_____

4. What were some of the things John was privileged to experience with Jesus?

_____

_____

5. Read Acts 3:1-11 and Acts 4:13. Explain the difference in John before and after Jesus was crucified.

_____

_____

### *Journey to the Father's Heart*

### *Part 1-Express Love to the Lord*

The Lord loves to hear us express our love to Him. Malachi 3:16 says, *"Then those who feared the LORD spoke with one another. The LORD paid attention and heard them and a book of remembrance was written before him of those who feared the LORD and esteemed his name."* [emphasis added]

Let's take some time and just verbally express our love to Jesus. Try to be creative and express yourself freely. If this is a new experience for you-if all you can say is "I love you Lord"-that is all right!

### *Part 2 – Be still and hear His affirming words*

Like prayer, adoration is meant to be a two-way conversation with the Lord. We speak and express our love and then we listen and hear Him speak. Psalm 46:10 says, "Be still and know that I am God." Now that you have expressed your love to Him, sit in stillness and allow yourself to hear His love for you. Imagine placing your head on Jesus bosom, like John, so you can hear His heart beat. It is during this time that the Lord may give you a scripture to read to affirm His love, a song of His love may come to mind, or you may hear Him whisper to you something like, "You are the apple of My eye" (Psalm 17:8).

**Journal what He says to you during this quiet time.**

_____

_____

_____

_____

_____

_____

_____

_____

_____

## *Part 3 – Repeat back the Word He has spoken*

Verbal repetition of a song, scripture, or His words allows what as spoken to resonate into the very depths of our soul. Additionally, speaking His word is a declaration of His love to us, which produces a deeper faith. Moreover, it declares to the powers of darkness that you are His child.

Practice lifting up words and songs of love to Him. (Don't worry how it sounds or if it rhymes). Then just sit in His presence and be still. Again, imagine putting your head on Jesus' bosom. Journal what you sense He is saying to you.

As mentioned earlier, bonding with your Heavenly Father is an important part of worshipping Him. Read these scriptures slowly, and meditate on who God is in your life.

**Bonding with the Father**
❖     **Psalm 36:5-10**
❖     **Ephesians 3:17-19**
❖     **Hosea 11:1, 3-4**
❖     **Zephaniah 3:17**

**Memorize:**

*"For I am convinced that neither death nor life, nor angels nor rulers, nor things present nor things to come, nor powers, neither height nor depth nor anything else in all creation, will be able to separate us from the love of God that is in Christ Jesus our Lord." Romans 8:38-39*

# Lesson 3 - A Date with Abba (Daddy)

*"But to all who did receive him, who believed in his name,*
*he gave the right to become children of God,"*
*John 1:12*

When my daughters were toddlers, they enjoyed a weekend ritual with their daddy. They would get up with their dad early in the morning, and he would make breakfast for them. His specialty was monkey shaped pancakes. As my daughters got older, we felt it would be a good idea for him to take each daughter out for a few hours on what became later known as a "daddy date." Once a month each of the girls would take turns going out to build their relationship with their dad. They would go to breakfast or to a special place of their choice. The girls always came back so excited! They looked forward to the next time they could go out with their daddy.

This was how the Lord began showing me the importance of going on "Daddy dates" with Him. He showed me that our daily time together was a time for both of us to get to know each other, have fun together, and build our relationship together. Having time with Abba (Daddy) did not come easy for me. It was hard to think of God as "my Daddy," as one would think of their earthly father. My first "Daddy date" was a time of all night prayer. After that prayer time, I did a study on the word "Abba." It is an Aramaic word which is a sign of unwavering trust and is equivalent to the English word for Daddy, an intimate word for Father.[2]

It may be hard to call the Lord of the Heavens "Daddy." Some may find it especially hard if they never had a good relationship with their earthly father. Whatever your situation, the Lord wants to have this level of intimacy with you, but for that to happen you must allow Him to break through any barriers you have so that He can be your Abba Father. What does this mean? It means allowing yourself to be open so you can experience the love of a Father unlike any love you have experienced before. For this to become a reality, you must first decide to put "self" and personal thoughts aside and be vulnerable in the presence of the Lord.

If you have struggled with past hurts from an earthly father, then this may be very difficult at first. But if you are consistent in allowing God to be your Abba, you will reap the benefits of love beyond your comprehension. Abba's love does not fail! We will be discussing more about how you can get rid of the pain from the past in the next section of this book. For now, let's go on a "Daddy date" and begin the journey of getting to know our Abba.

**Jesus, Son of God (Mark 1:1)**

Who better to follow on this journey than Jesus, the very Son of God! It was Jesus who first introduced the disciples to God as their Heavenly Father. Scripture shows us that Jesus spent most of His time with His Father, even while others were sleeping. His strength came from the time they spent together. The very attributes of His Father shaped his life. His countenance changed while in the presence of His Father.

**Read: Matthew 14:3, 10, 12-13, 23; Luke 9:28-36; John 14:6-11; John 1:12**

1.    What did Jesus do when he heard that John the Baptist was beheaded? _____

_____

2.    After ministry, Jesus often went to be with His Father. Why do you think he did so? _____

_____

3.    Where did Jesus take His disciples? _____

4.    In Luke 9:32, what happened to Peter and those with him? _____

_____

5.    What overshadowed them? _____

_____

6.    What did God say about Jesus? _____

_____

7.    How can we have access to the Father?

_____

_____

8.     How has the Father expressed His love to you?

_____

_____

9.     How does God see us?

_____

_____

_____

## *Journey to the Father's Heart*

Children are generally dependent upon their parents for everything they need which causes humility. Children cannot contribute to the needs of a family, but must trust their parents to provide for them in every way. Yet, Jesus blessed the children as they came to Him (Matthew 19:13-15). Jesus says that we are to be humble like little children. He taught his disciples that being self-centered and self-reliant was contrary to being a part of the kingdom of heaven. Being dependent upon their heavenly Daddy was what would make them great, not their deeds. He wanted them to realize they were arguing over petty issues instead of being humble (Matthew 18:1-4).

Let us pray:

*Precious Abba Father, I want to experience a greater measure of Your love and see myself as You see me. Please, open my heart and mind and heal me so we can see ourselves being fathered in perfect love by You. Lord, help us to come to You as a little child again, Amen.*

Play soft, worshipful music, close your eyes, and use your imagination to picture yourself as one of those children coming to Jesus. Picture Him placing His hands on you and blessing you.

As you spend time with Jesus as a little child, journal what you see and what you hear Him saying to your heart.

_____

_____

_____

_____

_____

_____

_____

_____

_____

_____

_____

_____

_____

_____

_____

_____

_____

_____

_____

_____

_____

_____

_____

Continue to lift up words and songs of love to Him. Just sit in His presence and be still. Imagine yourself as a young child, sitting on Jesus' lap – He is holding you. Journal what He says to you as you read the scriptures below and practice His presence.

If you can, go on a "Daddy date" with the Lord one day this week, even if it is just for a couple of hours. See if you can go to a cabin, a park, or a retreat center for a few hours. Journal your conversation with Abba.

Read these scriptures slowly, and meditate on who God is in your life.

**Bonding with the Father**
❖   **Jeremiah 3:19**
❖   **Psalm 89:26-29**
❖   **Roman 8:15-17**
❖   **Galatians 3:26-28**
❖   **Hebrews 12:9-11**

**Memorize:**

_"And he said, 'Abba, Father, all things are possible for you.'"_
_Mark 14:36a_

# Chapter 2

# Meditating on His Glory

# Lesson 4 - "Show me Your Glory"

*"Moses said, 'Please show me your glory.'"*
*Exodus 33:18*

One morning I was not able to have my quiet time with the Lord before leaving for work. So in the car on the way to work, I turned off the radio and began worshipping the Lord. I do not remember the ride to work because I was so caught up in the fellowship and communion we were having! That morning, the Lord brought to remembrance the passage in Exodus 33 where Moses asked to see God's glory. He wanted to see Him face to face and to experience more of God. This surprised me because Moses was closer to God than anyone during his time, yet he wanted more! He was not satisfied with what he had.

The more I meditated on this passage the more I began crying out, "Lord, show me Your glory. I don't want to miss seeing it." It was then that I asked myself, "Do I know what I am even asking? What is God's glory? How would I know it if I saw it? Surely it's more than a once-in-a-lifetime mountaintop experience!" God reveals Himself differently to each person throughout the scriptures. I decided I wanted my own experience, not the experience of Moses. My prayer became, "Lord, show me Your glory, however you want it to be – especially for me." It was then that the Lord took me through a study on "What is God's glory?"

In *Vine's Concise Dictionary*, "doxa" is the word used to define God's glory.[1] This word is explained as "the nature and acts of God in self manifestation; what He essentially is and does as exhibited in whatever way He reveals Himself in these respects, particularly in Christ. Supernatural, emanating from God (as in the 'Shekinah glory' in the pillar of cloud and Holy of Holies)."

After finding that definition, I knew what I was asking for. I not only wanted to see God manifest Himself naturally, but I also wanted to experience the Shekinah glory. This is the same glory that transformed both Moses and Jesus when they asked for His manifested glory to be revealed to, and through, them personally.

As I neared the end of my ride to work, I continued to worship the Lord. Then, suddenly, it was as if I heard the Lord say, "All who ask to see and experience My glory will." Sitting there, I felt as if the presence of the Lord was all through the van. All I could think about that entire day was my personal encounter with the Lord.

Driving home after work, I found myself being like Moses. I was asking for more. Driving along, I looked out over the shoreline of Lake Erie. The sun was setting through the clouds making them look fiery red. The waves of the water were crashing against the breaker wall so powerfully the water was showering across four lanes of traffic. I was thinking of the beauty of the scenery and the power of the waves when the Lord reminded me of Psalm 19:1-4, which says, *"THE HEAVENS declare the glory of God; and the firmament shows* and *proclaims His handiwork. Day after day pours forth speech, and night after night shows forth knowledge. There is no speech nor spoken word [from the stars]; their voice is not heard. Yet their voice [in evidence] goes out through all the earth, their sayings to the end of the world. Of the heavens has God made a tent for the sun,"* (AMPC) [emphasis added]

He also reminded me of Psalm 46:3-4 which says, *"Though its <u>waters roar and foam</u>, though the mountains tremble at its swelling. Selah. There is a river whose streams make glad the <u>city of God, the holy habitation of the Most High.</u>"* [emphasis added]

Again, the Lord revealed His glory! I was amazed at how quickly the Lord answered. It caused me to ask myself, "How much of God's glory and splendor have I missed?" I prayed, "Lord, continually keep my eyes open to the awesomeness and revelation of your glory."

**Moses - seeking God's Glory**

**Read Exodus 33:7-23**

1.  Why did Moses find such favor with God?

    _____

    _____

2.  How did Moses and God communicate?

    _____

    _____

3.  How do friends usually communicate with each other?

    _____

    _____

4.   Why do you think Moses asked to see the glory of God?

_____

_____

_____

5.   How is God's glory defined through this passage?

_____

_____

_____

6.   Is the type of relationship Moses had with God possible for you today?

_____

_____

7.   Are you experiencing this kind of intimate relationship with God? (Explain your answer).

_____

_____

_____

_____

*Journey to the Father's Heart*

Do you want to experience a greater measure of God's glorious presence? Let's take some time and ask Him.

*Dear Lord, I want to experience Your glory in the way that You have especially for me. Open my eyes wide to see all that You have for us. May I not miss a single opportunity to see You in a fresh new way. Lord, show me Your glory! Amen.*

Journal whatever you are seeing. Keep your eyes open throughout the day and write down all He shows you.

_____

_____

_____

_____

_____

_____

_____

_____

_____

_____

_____

_____

_____

_____

_____

_____

_____

_____

_____
_____
_____
_____
_____
_____
_____
_____
_____
_____
_____
_____
_____
_____

Continue to lift up words and songs of love to Him. Go on walks or sit near a body of water. Go to a park and just sit in His presence. Journal what He says to you as you read the scriptures below.

**Bonding with the Father**
❖    **Exodus 16:10**
❖    **Exodus 25:22**
❖    **Exodus 34:5-7**
❖    **Exodus 40:34-38**

**Memorize:**

_"Moses said, 'Please show me your glory.'" Exodus 33:18_

# Lesson 5 – Promise of His Glory

*"And those whom He predestined, He also called; and those whom He called, He also justified [declared free of the guilt of sin]; and those whom He justified, He also glorified [raising them to a heavenly dignity]."*
*Romans 8:30 (AMP)*

The more I became aware of His glory, the more I wanted. I was hungry for more of His fullness and love. I became consumed with the thought that if Moses and the apostles were just mere humans like me, surely all that was given to them was also what He intended for me. I continued my study on the Shekinah glory and the transformation process that happened to Jesus. *Vine's Bible Dictionary* defines the word "transfigure" as *metamorphoo,* meaning "to change into another form." It's the same word used in Romans 12:2 "Do not be conformed to this world, but be <u>transformed</u> by the renewal of your mind, that by testing you may discern what is the will of God, what is good and acceptable and perfect." [emphasis added] To undergo a complete change under the power of God requires a different expression in character and conduct. It is both an inward (character) and an outward (physical) change. [2]

This confirmed that what I wanted was also God's desire for my life. It is an attainable thing meant for all His children. The disciples received this transformation in the upper room on the Day of Pentecost. Jesus commanded them to "wait for the promise of the Father" (Acts 1:4). The promise was the Holy Spirit Himself.

It was during one of my "Daddy dates" that extended over a weekend that the Lord reminded me of a dream I had several years prior. In the dream, I was looking in a mirror, but I could not make out my face. I tried on several masks, and even though they made me look good, none of them seemed to fit me. I still could not make out the image of who I was. Then in my dream, the Lord took me to what looked like a cocoon and showed me the inside of it. He asked me if I was willing to go inside. He promised He would not leave me and when I emerged, I would be changed into a beautiful butterfly. He said He wanted to put me in there so He could mold me and shape me. Then when I emerged, I would not have to wear all the uncomfortable masks; I could be who He created me to be.

It was during this special weekend that I realized the Lord was preparing me for more of His transforming love. The Father assigns this work of transformation to the Holy Spirit. Even though I had been saved for years and grew up in an evangelical church, the Holy Spirit as a person was rarely taught. As I began to study this, I realized that it was only through the work of the Holy Spirit that this transformation could happen. Acts 1:8 says, "but you will receive power when the Holy Spirit has come upon you, and you will be my witnesses in Jerusalem and in all Judea and Samaria, and to the end of the earth." Like the disciples, I was baptized with water but I wanted the baptism of the Holy Spirit (Acts 1:5), to be transformed into Christ-likeness, so that all who saw me would be *"amazed and see I was an ordinary person who had been transformed with Jesus."* (Acts 4:13) [emphasis added]

2 Corinthians 3:18 says, *"And we all, with unveiled face, beholding the glory of the Lord, are being transformed into the same image from one degree of glory to another. For this comes from the Lord who is the Spirit."* [emphasis added] One man, Moses, was the only one to see the Lord face to face (Exodus 33:11). Now because of Jesus, "all of us" have access. Moses kept his face veiled before the Israelites because of their fear (Exodus 34:30-35). But because Jesus paid the price we no longer have anything to fear - so we can let our faces reflect His glory for all to see.

## The Transfiguration of Jesus

### Read Matthew 17:1-13 & Luke 9:28-36

1.    Where does Jesus take the disciples?

_____

_____

2.    Which disciples did Jesus take with him?

_____

_____

3.    What was their purpose for going there?

_____

4.    What started to happen to Jesus as he prayed?

_____

5.    Who appeared with Jesus?

_____

6.    What did the voice from the cloud say?

_____

_____

7.    How did the disciples react when they saw all this transpire?

_____

_____

### *Journey to the Father's Heart*

Before your start today's journey, pray the prayer below. Read Revelation 4 and begin to imagine what His glory looks like.

*Lord, I want to be transformed into your likeness. I want to exchange my heart and mind for your heart and mind. I want to be changed from glory to glory. Lord, may I be a mirror that brightly reflects your glory. I know this can only be accomplished as the Holy Spirit works within me. So, Holy Spirit, baptize me! I want to be filled with your fullness. Go deep within all the dark areas of my soul and expose them so that I can begin to be transformed to reflect your glory even more. In Jesus' Holy Name, Amen.*

Continue to practicing coming into His presence and worshipping Him. Write to Him below, and tell him how much you want more of Him and less of you. As you read the following scriptures, use your imagination to place yourself as one of the apostles who was with Jesus on the mountain.

Journal what is on your heart.

_____

_____

_____

_____

_____

_____

_____

_____

_____

_____

_____

_____

_____

_____

_____

_____

_____

_____

_____

_____

_____

_____

_____

_____

_____

_____

_____

_____

_____

_____

_____

_____

_____

_____

_____

_____

_____

_____

_____

_____

Read these scriptures slowly and meditate on who God is in your life.

**Bonding with the Father**
- ❖ **Acts 1 & 2**
- ❖ **Acts 9**
- ❖ **Philippians 3:4-11**
- ❖ **Revelation 21**

## Memorize:

_"And those whom He predestined He also called, and those whom He called He also justified, and those whom He justified He also glorified." Romans 8:30_

# Lesson 6 – Whole Earth be Filled with His Glory

*"May the Whole Earth be filled with His Glory."*
*Psalm 72:19*

Do you ever wonder what would it look like to have God's manifested glory with us today? Would we even recognize it? In the New Testament, the Jewish people had been waiting for the coming of the Messiah, and even when He was walking among them, they did not recognize Him. The priests had become so arrogant in their head knowledge of the coming Messiah that they lacked personal relationship with Him. Intimacy with Christ was not intended to be for a select few like Moses, Elijah, or the prophets, but for all.

Even today, there are many in our churches that know the scriptures and have accepted Christ as Savior but of their own choosing have failed to enter the fullness of the relationship the Lord wants with them. Failing to recognize His glory now will cause us to miss or, even worse, be rejected at the second coming.

Jesus warns of this very thing in Matthew 7:21-23, *"Not everyone who says to Me, Lord, Lord, will enter the kingdom of heaven, but he who does the will of My Father Who is in heaven. Many will say to Me on that day, Lord, Lord, have we not prophesied in Your name and driven out demons in Your name and done many mighty works in Your name? And then I will say to them openly (publicly), I never knew you; depart from Me, you who act wickedly [disregarding My commands].* (AMPC) [emphasis added]

The word "knew" in this passage means intimately and personally. It implies an active relationship, not just as Savior but also as friend. It is the same word used to convey union between a man and a woman.[3] The only way we can recognize the glory of the Lord is to be like Moses and spend time in His presence getting to know Him...intimately. To practice being in His presence is to be like Peter, James, and John: to sit and behold His glory (Luke 9:34). Because Christ dwells in us, and as we continue to grow and change, we will increasingly know His glory. As we come into His presence we will be able to comprehend His glory, and, like the three disciples, we will be transformed so that we can reveal His glory to the world. Imagine the earth filled with His glory before His coming!

In the Old Testament, God's glory led the Israelites in a cloud as it hovered over the tabernacle. After the temple was built, Solomon prayed and the glory of the Lord filled the temple and became a continuous fire on the altar (2 Chronicles 7:1-3, 16). The continuing sin of the Israelites and their unwillingness to repent caused God's glory to leave the temple just as Ezekiel prophesied it would (Ezekiel 8-11). It didn't return until Christ Himself came to represent the Glory of His Father (Hebrews 1:3). After His ascension, the Shekinah glory came upon the disciples on the day of Pentecost as tongues of fire to reside within each disciple (Acts 2:3). Paul writes in 1 Corinthians 3:16, "Do you not know that you are God's temple and that God's Spirit dwells in you?"

We are the temple of God; the Shekinah glory is for us today. The only way to receive this is to come into the presence of God Himself so that the flame of the Holy Spirit can continuously burn on the altar of our hearts. This is how the whole earth can be filled with His glory.

**The Son reflects His Father's Glory:**

Jesus reflects the Glory of His Father and we are called to do the same. Read on about how Jesus did this and learn how you can reflect the Father's glory just as Jesus did.

**Read John 1:14 & John 17**

1.    In John 1:14 whose glory have we seen?

_____

_____


2.    In John 17, how did Jesus bring forth His Father's glory?

_____

_____


3.    In John 17:10 what did Jesus mean when He said, "They are my glory" or "Glory has come to me through them"?

_____

_____

4.    According to this chapter, did the disciples also receive the Lord's glory?  How?

_____

_____

5.    Why did Jesus give the disciples His glory?

_____

_____

6.    What must we do to have the glory of the Lord in us?

_____

_____

### *Journey to the Father's Heart*

Pray from your heart the following prayer, then read Revelation 19:1-10 and meditate on God's glory.

*Dear Lord,*

*I desire to reflect Your glory on this earth. Just as You have created the world to give You glory, You have also created me for Your glory. Show me how I can bring You glory.  Help me to be willing to die to all that robs You of glory.  Father, through your Holy Spirit, show me what those things are.  In Jesus Name, Amen.*

**Write if there is anything God reveals that robs you of more of his glory. Feel free to add more of your heart to this prayer. Journal your desires and then listen to God's heart.**

_____

_____

_____

_____

_____

_____

_____

_____

_____

_____

_____

_____

**Bonding with the Father**
- ❖ **1 Corinthians 10:31**
- ❖ **Ephesians 1:17-18**
- ❖ **1 Peter 5:4**
- ❖ **2 Chronicles 7:1-3, 16**
- ❖ **Ezekiel chapters 8-11**

*Memorize:*

*"To them God chose to make known how great among the Gentiles are the riches of the glory of this mystery, which is Christ in you, the hope of glory." Colossians 1:27*

# Chapter 3

# Journaling His Love

# Lesson 7 – The Invitation

*"But he said to him, 'A man once gave a great banquet and invite many.'"*
*Luke 14:16*

Imagine you just received an invitation to come to the King's court to be part of a special celebration that is to take place within the hour. You feel honored to have received an invitation, but you wonder if this could be a mistake because the King has never invited you before. Choosing not to question it any further for fear you will talk yourself out of it, you plan to attend. You immediately go and change into your best clothes. Shortly afterward you find yourself outside the door of the castle and take one last look at your clothing.

You look down and to your dismay the clothes you are wearing, all of the sudden, look torn and tattered. To your horror, before you can run off, the door opens and the man at the door asks for your invitation. He welcomes you in without a single comment about your clothing. He walks you down a long corridor toward an entrance that is covered by a large, red velvet curtain. As you walk, you can hear music and cymbals and shouts of praise growing ever louder as you approach. The man walks through the entrance expecting you to follow, but all you can do is peek through the curtain. The man proceeds to the front of a huge ballroom.

In the front of the ballroom, there are two thrones and behind them is a chorus resonating beautiful music. There are dancers in front of the thrones, which partially block your view.

Periodically as the dancers move about, you catch glimpses of The King and His Son sitting on the thrones. You scan the room and see thousands of other people, bowed low on their knees, worshipping the King and His Son. Feeling this is what you should be doing, you come from behind the curtain and look for a space on the floor.

You feel safe entering because all eyes are on the King and His Son. You figure that if you can get to a spot quickly enough and bow down no one will see you. You quickly enter the room, kneel on the ground, and keep your face buried in your hands. After a few minutes, out of curiosity, you decide to peek through your fingers, and to your horror, you notice the dancers have parted; walking towards you down the center of the aisle created by the dancers is the King's Son!

You continue to keep your face hidden in hopes that you will not be noticed, but soon you feel a presence standing over you and a voice calling your name. "Yes?" you meekly answer, keeping your head down and your face buried. Then you feel a hand on your shoulder as He kneels beside you and says, "Come with Me."

You utter, "Oh, please my Lord, I am not worthy - please do not look at me, for I am unclean." He then takes your hands from your face and gently pulls you to stand upright. He places His hands under your chin, looks you in the eyes and says, "You are perfect." As soon as He says this, you look down and your old tattered clothes have become beautiful, white wedding clothes! He takes your hand and says, "Thank you for accepting my invitation."

You walk together, hand in hand, into another room. It is just as large as the first, but there is a long banqueting table there which runs the entire length of the room. It is set with lit candles, white linen table clothes, white china plates and crystal glasses. People are already sitting at the table and there are two seats left - one at the far end of the table and another directly to its right. He continues to hold your hand and walks you to the last seat on the corner. As you walk everyone stares at you in awe. Before you sit down, He announces to those at the table, "This is my beloved." As you sit together you ask him, "Why me? I do not understand." He smiles at you and says, *"I brought you to my banqueting table and my banner over you is love."* (Song of Solomon 2:4) [emphasis added]

You see Christ wants us to see ourselves as He sees us. We are His bride and He is the Bridegroom. Although we dress ourselves daily in our outside clothes, they can't hide what is really happening on in the inside, where our lives are really tattered and torn; but what we perceive as rags, He redeems as beauty. Don't get me wrong - in comparison to Him our sins are but filthy rags. But once we come to Him and repent and accept Him as Lord over our lives, He no longer sees us that way. We are washed clean and are a new creation! (2 Corinthians 5:17)

Some of us live with so many labels given to us by others that we look at ourselves from their perspective. These false images are purposely thrown at us by the enemy and teach us to hate the very image of Christ that we are meant to reflect. We are created in the image of Christ, and if the enemy can destroy that, he can destroy the purposes we have in Christ. The Lord wants to change the false image we have, not only of ourselves, but also of Him. In studying the characteristics of Christ, we begin to perceive the truth and begin to see ourselves as He sees us. In this story, Christ was King and Bridegroom. That makes us princesses and brides! It is my prayer as you do today's lesson that you will develop a new level of intimacy with Christ. I pray that this will result in a holy consummation which will give birth to a new reality in Christ.

**The Bride of Christ**

Throughout scripture we are called the bride of Christ, yet it is hard for many of us to imagine ourselves as being wed to the Lord. As you read these passages you will learn to personalize them so that you will be able to see yourself as He sees you.

**Read Psalm 45 & Hosea 2:14-20**

1.    As you read Psalm 45, write out the attributes of Christ that are revealed in this passage.

_____

_____

_____

_____

_____

_____

2.    Who has blessed and anointed the King?

_____

_____

_____

3.	As the Bride of Christ what is expected of you? (Psalm 45:10-11)

_____

_____


4.	According to the rest of Psalm 45 how does Christ see you?

_____

_____

_____


5.	In Hosea, the Lord uses a lot of allegories to describe his plans for His bride. Ask the Lord how these apply to you and write your thoughts.

_____

_____

_____

_____


### *Journey to the Father's Heart*

Begin by reading Psalm 45 again. Afterward, close your eyes and imagine yourself in the throne room of the Lord. Using the attributes you found in the above passages begin worshipping Him with words of love and adoration.

*Oh, my King and my Lord, how we worship You and declare You King of Kings and Lord of Lords! What an awesome privilege to be invited into Your courts and to praise You.*

*Thank you for Your invitation to Your banqueting table, and most of all for Your love. Amen.*

### Journal your desires and then listen for God's voice

_____

_____

_____

_____

_____

_____

_____

_____

_____

_____

_____

_____

_____

_____

_____

_____

_____

_____

_____

_____

_____

_____

_____

_____

_____

_____

_____

_____

_____

_____

_____

_____

_____

## Bonding with the Father
- ❖ **John 3:29**
- ❖ **Revelation 21:2, 9**
- ❖ **Isaiah 62:5**
- ❖ **Revelation 19:7-9**
- ❖ **Song of Solomon 2:1-4**

## Memorize and personalize:

*"Hear, O daughter, and consider, and incline your ear: forget your people and your father's house, and the king will desire your beauty. Since he is your lord, bow to him.*
*Psalm 45:10-11*

# Lesson 8 - The Pursuit

*"You will seek me and find Me when you seek Me with all*
*your heart."*
*Jeremiah 29:13*

In the last lesson, you discovered the love our King has for His bride. At some point in your life you accepted the invitation to let Jesus into your heart to rule and to reign. But do you realize that He chose you, long before you were even born? This is clearly revealed in the following scriptures:

*"Before I formed you in the womb I knew you, and before*
*you were born I consecrated you."* Jeremiah 1:5a

*"even as he chose us in him before the foundation of the*
*world, that we should be holy and blameless before him. In*
*love, he predestined us for adoption through Jesus Christ,*
*according to the purpose of his will,"* Ephesians 1:4-5
[emphasis added]

What an awesome thought! We didn't really come to Him; He was pursuing us, waiting patiently until the day we would lay down our lives and follow Him!

Although the Lord first pursued us as we learned to walk and hear Him speak to us, there are times we may struggle in hearing Him. It's because he wants us to learn to pursue Him. It's when we continue the pursuit that the heart grows closer to the Lord. Jesus even said to His disciples, "Come, follow me" (Matthew 4:19). David in Psalm 63:8 says, "My soul follows close behind you; your right hand upholds me" (NKJV). Some definitions of "follow" to consider are "impinge, cling, or adhere to; follow close by pursuit, pursue hard."[1] He pursued us and now it is up to us to pursue hard after Him.

We as a culture have grown accustomed to chasing after many things, even as Christians. But we are called to desire only one thing, and that is the Lord. In Matthew 22:37 *And He said to him, "You shall love the Lord your God with all your heart and with all your soul and with all your mind."* [emphasis added] This is a whole body, mind, and spirit experience. It's not just heady knowledge of His Word; it must become experiential. Love is a verb - it is meant to show action. The very word God uses for love is agape.[2] Agape love can only be known by the action it prompts. God's action was through the perfect expression of the Lord Jesus Christ who was given to us for our salvation. The Bible, His Word, is a long list of the expressions of His love. To contain God's love only in our heads, and not also in our hearts, results in a puffed-up religion - not an intimate relationship.

To pursue Christ and follow hard after Him involves faith, emotion, passion, and zeal. It takes all our senses, and, at times, all our strength. It's not a matter of striving because that involves frustration. We don't have to win His love or acceptance; we already have His unlimited love. Pursuing Him involves us opening our hearts to receive His love and increasing our capacity to take in the abundant love He has to give. Pursuing Him means always wanting more of His Love and never being satisfied or content with what we have. The more we take in, the more we become receivers of His love, and the more that love pours out of us to others.

## Pursuing Christ

So, what must we do to show our love to Christ?

We must continue our pursuit of Him.

When we begin to pursue Christ, we begin an exciting journey of discovering the magnitude of His love. This love becomes experiential and not just a religious homage. In Mark 5:25-34 we read about the woman who suffered from constant bleeding. She knew Christ was the only one that could heal her. She thought "If I could just get to Jesus.... but how can I get to Him?" The immense crowds kept her from Him. Even though she knew she was considered "unclean", she pushed her way through the crowds surrounding Jesus, and finally she grabbed a hold of the hem of His garment. Jesus stopped because He felt power go out of Him and asked, "Who touched me?" The disciples looked around and told Jesus the crowd was all around Him, and it could have been anyone. But Jesus turned and saw the woman, who by now was trembling on her knees because she knew what had just happened to her...she had been healed! Jesus came up to her, looked her in the eyes and told her, "Be of good cheer, daughter, your faith has made you well. Go in peace and be healed of your affliction." And scripture says she was made well from that hour. She becomes known as the only woman in scripture that Jesus addresses as "daughter." When we make an effort to pursue Him, He returns the gesture and touches us.

## Read: Ephesians 3:14-19 & Song of Solomon 3:1-4

In the Ephesians passage, Paul is praying for the believers in Ephesus to have a greater understanding of the Father's love. Let's look at these verses:

1.    Every family is named after whom?

_____

2.    Because of the adoption what is it that we are granted? Where? (v. 16)

_____

3.    Christ dwells in your _____
through _____.

4.    What does it mean to be rooted in love?

_____

_____

5.    What happens when a plant's roots are weak or not planted deep enough in the proper soil?

_____

_____

6.    As you begin to pursue and _____ the love of Christ you will begin to be _____ with the _____ of God. (v. 19)

7.    When did the Beloved begin to seek the one she loved? (Song of Solomon 3:1-4)

_____

_____

8.    What happened when she couldn't find him?

_____

_____

9.    Did she give up? _____

10.    Once she caught up to him what did she do?

_____

_____

### *Journey to the Father's Heart*

Begin by reading Mark 5:25-34 then close your eyes and imagine yourself being the woman who was desperate for healing from Jesus: I know for some this may be difficult but keep pursing and pushing through the crowd. Become like the Beloved who is desperately seeking the one you love.

*Let's pray: Oh Lord, as the deer pants for streams of water, so my soul pants for you, O God. My soul thirsts for you, God. I will keep pursuing You because I want to see Your face. It is You I want; no one else will do. No one can touch my heart as you can. Amen.*

# Journal your desires and then listen

_____

_____

_____

_____

_____

_____

_____

_____

_____

_____

_____

_____

_____

_____

_____

_____

**Bonding with the Father**
❖ **Isaiah 26:8-9**
❖ **Proverbs 3:5-6**
❖ **I John 3:1-2**
❖ **Psalm 63:1-8**

**Memorize and personalize:**

*"You will seek me and find me, when you seek me with all your heart," Jeremiah 29:13*

# Lesson 9 - Abiding in His Love

*"If you keep My commandments, you will abide in My love, just as I have kept My Father's commandments and abide in His love."*
*John 15:10*

In the previous lesson, you captured the Heart of the Lover of your soul! You have been faithful to pursue Him and show Him how desperately you truly desire Him. You have fought against those things that would try to rob you of your time with Him and by doing so you have captured His attention. He takes you by the hand and says, "abide **in** my love" (John 15:9). The word "abide" means "stay in a given place, state, relation, or expectancy."[3] It is a state of being. In order to abide or remain in His love you must have a conscious acknowledgement of where you are at all times. Anything outside of abiding in His love is being outside of His will. Galatians 5:16 states, "I say then: Walk in the Spirit, and you shall not fulfill the lust of the flesh." (NKJV)

You see, as Christians, when we accept Christ as Savior, our life no longer is our own. Scripture says we were "bought with a price" (1 Corinthians 7:23). Keep repeating this until it sinks in: "My life is not my own. My life is not my own." We think that Christ comes into our lives and so lives in us. We visualize a "big us" and a "little Him" living inside of us. We need to reverse that and visualize ourselves as "small" and Christ as "big". In reality, we are living **IN** Him. Christ is not only in you - He is above and below you, and in front of you, and behind you and on both sides of you (Psalm 139:5). I asked the Lord to show me what this looks like and He showed me a picture of a person walking, surrounded by a bubble. He is not only in us, but He is also around us.

I believe we all limit God and put Him in a box because we have a false image of the magnitude and power He represents. (The Israelites were guilty of this too.) When we do this, we put limits on what He can do through us. One day, the Lord gave me this scripture in Psalm 78:41 that helped me put this into perspective: *"Yes, again and again they tempted God, And limited the Holy One of Israel."* (NKJV) [emphasis added]

Did you ever make potholders as a child? Remember how you would stretch colored bands across the board and attach them to the pegs at each end? Then you would turn the board and weave individual colored bands in and out of the stationary bands, attaching each new band to the pegs at either end, until a tightly woven square was produced. We are meant to have the very essence of Christ woven into our being so that we can function as He created us, to do His Will on earth as it is in heaven.

**Abide in My Love**

In John 15:5, you will see that we are to be connected to the vine so closely that *"apart from Me you can do nothing."* [emphasis added] In other words, the only way we could lose that bubble of His presence around us is to be disobedient to what He says we are to do. John 15:10 says, *"If you keep My commandments, you will abide in My love, just as I have kept My Father's commandments and abide in His love."* [emphasis added] It is as simple as hearing and obeying. This is why we have been learning to listen and hear from our Heavenly Father. We must be careful, though, that we do not become like the Israelites who hardened their hearts when they heard God speak.

**Read John 15:1-16 and answer the following:**

1.   Who is the vine? Who is the vinedresser?

_____

_____

2.   What does the Father do to the branches that do not bear fruit?

_____

_____

3.   What does He do to the ones who that do bear fruit?

_____

_____

4.   How can you bear fruit?

_____

_____

5.   From our reading, what does abide mean?

_____

_____

_____

6. How can we abide in His love? (v. 10)

_____

_____

7. What are His commandments? (v. 12)

_____

_____

8. As we abide in His love what do we receive from Him? (v. 11)

_____

_____

_____

9. Who chose us and why? (v. 16)

_____

_____

_____

### *Journey to the Father's Heart:*

Today we learned abide means to stay or remain in His presence with expectancy. Let's begin today's journey by not asking anything of Him. Our goal today is to simply worship Him. Choose a song, a scripture verse or just begin speaking words of love and adoration to Him. No agenda, no asking - just loving on Him and praising His name.

*Let's pray:*

*Father, we thank You so much that You love us. We thank You that You prune us! You have chosen us to be Your children and to receive glory through us. So, Father, be blessed as we exalt Your name today! You are truly all that we need. Nothing else compares to You and Your love. (Continue adoring your Heavenly Father.)*

After your worship time ask the Lord to show you how you need to abide more in Him. Ask Him if there is any disobedience that is preventing you from being in the bubble of His presence. Confess this as sin and choose to turn and walk in obedience so that you can remain in His presence.

**Listen and journal what He says!**

_____

_____

_____

_____

_____

_____

_____

_____

_____

_____

_____

_____

_____

_____
_____
_____
_____
_____
_____
_____
_____
_____
_____
_____
_____
_____
_____
_____

## Bonding with the Father
❖ **Psalm 15**
❖ **Psalm 91:1-2**
❖ **1 John 2:6**
❖ **1 John 4:12-16**

## Memorize:

*"Now he who keeps His commandments abides in Him, and He in him. And by this we know that He abides in us, by the Spirit whom He has given us." 1 John 3:24* (NKJV)

# Section II – The Inward Journey

# Journey into the Depths of our Hearts

# Journey into the Depths of our Hearts

In the first part of our journey we learned to bond with Our Heavenly Abba. As our journey continues, we will now allow Him to go deeper into our hearts. Scripture says we are to "rend our hearts, and not our garments" Joel 2:13 (NKJV). It is here that we make the sacrifice of giving the Lord total control of every aspect of our being. We will allow Him to take us into the very depths of our inner-being as He begins to uncover, ever so gently, those areas of hurt, pain and sin that keep us from a deeper level of intimacy. On this part of the journey we must give the Lord permission to clear out the dark closet of our heart so that we may able to comprehend in our spirit the deeper things of the Lord.

The following scripture tells us that our minds are unable to fully comprehend the fullness of the Lord. It is only with the help of the Holy Spirit, who dwells within us once we have accepted Christ, that we can comprehend the things of Christ. 1 Corinthians 2:10-12 says, "But God has revealed *them* to us through His Spirit. For the Spirit searches all things, yes, even the deep things of God. For what man knows the things of a man except the spirit of the man which is in him? Even so no one knows the thoughts of God except the Spirit of God. Now we have received, not the spirit of the world, but the Spirit who is from God, that we may know the things that have been freely given to us by God." (NKJV)

God created man as a three part being: body, soul, and spirit. Our soul is comprised of our heart (emotions), our mind (intellect), and our will. The soul is also the place from where our character and personality emanate. God wants to activate our "spiritual heart" so that we can begin to hear and understand the things of the Lord. It is our heart that was designed to communicate with the Lord.

It is only when we seek the Lord with our whole heart, and not our mind, that we will have a greater revelation of who He is. Ephesians 3:16-19 says that "He would grant you, according to the riches of His glory, to be strengthened with might through His Spirit in the inner man, that Christ may dwell in your hearts through faith; that you, being rooted and grounded in love, may be able to comprehend with all the saints what *is* the width and length and depth and height- to know the love of Christ which passes knowledge; that you may be filled with all the fullness of God." (NKJV) [emphasis added].

In the journey upward we sought His heart by intellectually getting to know His character. In the journey inward we will seek His face intimately. Intimacy is defined in this journey as *"IN-TO-ME-HE-SEES."*

Have you ever had someone gaze deeply into your eyes? We often avoid this uncomfortable situation because we are afraid he will see something in us that is unpleasant. Our eyes are the gateway to our soul. When God gazes into our eyes, the masks we wear, whether known or unknown, begin to come off. All of the shame, guilt, and pain that we have been hiding are suddenly exposed by God's loving gaze. And then a miraculous thing happens: these past hurts are exchanged for a greater measure of His love. It is not that He suddenly loves us more, but that we suddenly learn to trust Him more and allow more of His love into our hearts.

I know that you may have a hard time with some of these exercises because it may bring up painful memories. You may have been abused, mistreated, or ignored by others in your past. You may be blaming someone for the problems you have today because of pain you experienced in your past. It is time to stop "the blame-game" and take responsibility for how we react to situations. Now is the time to learn how to lay these things at the foot of the cross of Jesus so your relationship with our Heavenly Father can grow deeper. Ultimately, it comes down to your willingness to exchange your pain for His love. If you truly are faithful to work through these things, God will do an amazing work in you!

Here are some key verses for this part of the journey that you may need to hold on to:

Isaiah 53:5 *"But He was wounded for our transgressions,* He was *bruised for our iniquities; the chastisement for our peace* was *upon Him, and by His stripes we are healed."* (NKJV) [emphasis added].

Isaiah 43:18-19 *"Do not remember the former things; Or ponder the things of the past. Listen carefully, I am about to do a new thing! Now it will spring forth; will you not be aware of it? I will even put a road in the wilderness, Rivers in the desert.* (AMP) [emphasis added].

2 Corinthian 5:17-19 *"Therefore if anyone* is *in Christ,* he is *a new creation; old things have passed away; behold, all things have come become new. Now all things* are *of God, who has reconciled us to Himself through Jesus Christ, and has given us the ministry of reconciliation, that is, that God was in Christ reconciling the world to Himself, not imputing their*

*trespasses to them, and has committed to us the word of reconciliation.* " (NKJV) [emphasis added].

If this part of the journey gets difficult for you, come back to this page to meditate upon and pray through these scriptures until you feel God's peace and presence. He will be faithful to walk with you on this journey!

# Chapter 4

# Opening Our Hearts

# Lesson 10 - Submitting to His Lordship

*"So therefore, any one of you who does not renounce all that*
*he has cannot be my disciple."*
*Luke 14:33*

For us to understand His Lordship we must understand ruler-ship in a monarch led society. This is difficult to comprehend by citizens of the USA because we have a democratic government elected by the people and rules for the people. But in a society run by a monarch, everything is about and for that person, not about the people. In essence, everything is possessed and owned by the king. The people of the kingdom work to serve the king and his interests; their whole lives are centered around the king. Even the type of work they do is centered on serving in, and maintaining, the kingdom. Submitting to this type of ruler-ship as a Christian is a choice, but as a disciple it is not. As a disciple, submission is required. Thayer Dictionary defines "disciple" as a "learner, pupil, disciple."[1]

There are a lot of people who call themselves Christians, but they have never made God "Lord" over every area of their lives; making Him "Lord" means giving Him total control. This includes giving up control of things like our finances and our time. It is not about what we want; it's all about Him. Even coming to Him in worship needs to be about Him and Him alone. It is not about what we can get <u>from</u> Him; it's what we can do <u>for</u> Him.

We in the church have done many a disfavor when we have led people to the Lord using a rote memory "sinner's prayer." We use this "sales tactic" to get them into the Kingdom and then allow them to think that God is here to make their life on earth easier. We can't sugar coat the gospel; we need to be cautious about telling people that all their problems will go away the moment they accept Christ. This is why many people turn their back on Christ - because they didn't get what they expected out of the relationship. Coming to God cannot be like coming to a Santa Claus, whereby being "good" you will get what you want. Our obedience and submission to God is what proves our love for Him, but when we are tested many of us fail. Society teaches us that life is all about feeling good and the pursuit of happiness. We equate that to receiving the things we want. This is a twisted principle that causes many Christians to stumble and wander away from God. In reality, once we invite God into a situation and allow Him to take control, change can happen.

**There is a Price to Pay**

Those who choose to submit to his Lordship have a price to pay:

"Now great crowds accompanied him, and he turned and said to them, 'If anyone comes to me and does not hate his own father and mother and wife and children and brothers and sisters, yes, and even his own life, he cannot be my disciple. Whoever does not bear his own cross and come after me cannot be my disciple. So therefore, any one of you who does not renounce all that he has cannot be my disciple.'" Luke 14:25-27 & 33

We must realize that we are faced with a choice; we are never pressured - just loved. But we can no longer go through life as we once did; we need to choose who will be in control of our lives, and who, or what, we will obey. Let me show you another passage that may help you:

*"Not everyone who says to me, 'Lord, Lord,' will enter the kingdom of heaven, but the one who does the will of My Father who is in heaven. On that day many will say to me, 'Lord, Lord, did we not prophesy in your name, and cast out demons in your name, and do many mighty works in your name?' And then will I declare to them, 'I never knew you; depart from me, you workers of lawlessness."* Matthew 7: 21-23 [emphasis added]

The word "knew" in the passage above means to know intimately, not just an intellectual knowledge but to know someone much like a man and wife know each other.[2] The issue is that some have called Jesus "Lord" yet many have not given Him Lordship over their whole life, and this is disobedience to the Heavenly Father. This even applies to those who seem spiritual and have performed miracles. We need to be on guard that we don't just look spiritual but have permission from the Lord to do what we think we are to do.

**Submitting to His Lordship**

Even while He was here on earth, Jesus submitted to the Father in complete obedience. He realized His life was not His own and that He only did what He saw the Father doing. Being a true disciple means you are willing to be one who learns, and that requires being teachable and submitted to another. Fully submitting to Jesus changes your relationship

109

with Him. He is no longer just your Savior; He becomes Lord of your life.

As I mentioned earlier in this lesson, your life is not your own; you have been bought with a price. Jesus died a horrible death to give you abundant life here and eternal life later. You were purchased by His blood. He is your master, and you are now His willing slave.

**Read and answer the following questions:**

**Matthew 19:16-30 & Luke 9:57-62**

1.    In Matthew 19:16 what does the rich man call Jesus?

_____

_____

(Note: By calling Jesus "Good Master" he is giving Him a title of teacher, but not one of ruler.)

2.    What deed did Jesus tell him he must do?

_____

_____

Does this mean that we must sell all our possessions? No; but it does mean we should not allow these things take precedence in our lives.

3.    Is there anything you would not give up for Jesus?

_____

_____

4.    If not by works, how can we get into heaven? v. 26

_____

_____


5.    In Luke 9:57 another young man made a promise to follow Jesus wherever He would go. What was Christ's request to this young man?

_____

_____


6.    What were the issues that the other two men had about following Jesus?

_____

_____


7.    There is a cost to following Christ. What would it cost you to follow Him?

_____

_____


### In-to- Me- He- Sees; The Journey Inward

It's time to ask the Lord what areas of your Life you need to surrender. Has He just been a Savior to you? If so, now is the time to allow him to be Lord of all.

*My Adoni (Lord and Master),*

*I realize I have come to you expecting only to receive from you. I have placed conditions on my love towards you. Please forgive me for not being satisfied with just being near You. I also realize there are areas of my life that I am still holding on to. I want to hand these areas over to You now. I want to give You complete and total access to my life. I no longer consider my life my own. It is Yours to do with it as You please. Please reveal any areas of my life\* that I need to surrender control to You, or areas in which I have not trusted You. Amen.*

\*Take some time to write these areas down. Once you've finished, imagine yourself at the foot of the cross and place each one of these things there. Pray a prayer of release for each item then journal what you experience.

_____

_____

_____

_____

_____

_____

_____

_____

_____

_____

_____

_____

_____
_____
_____
_____
_____
_____
_____
_____
_____
_____
_____
_____
_____
_____
_____
_____
_____
_____

**Bonding with the Father; He is Jehovah (self existent one, Adonai, Lord and Master)**
- ❖ **Deuteronomy 10:17**
- ❖ **Psalm 16:2**
- ❖ **Psalm 105:1-7**
- ❖ **Romans 14:7-9**
- ❖ **1 Corinthians 6:19-20**

**Memorize:**

*"So therefore, any one of you who does not renounce all that he has cannot be My disciple." Luke 14:33*

# Lesson 11 - Da-masc-us

*"Now as he went on his way, he approached Damascus, and suddenly a light from heaven flashed around him."*
*Acts 9:3*

After our church's first "Weekend of Prayer" in 2001, I came home and couldn't sleep. The Lord began showing me my true self. It was as if He held a mirror up to my face. I realized I was "playing church" - hiding behind a myriad of masks - not letting anyone see the real me inside. Fear was gripping my heart; I didn't want anyone to see that I was in emotional pain. That night I wept mightily before the Lord. He ministered to me through various visions, showing me all the walls I had put up around me and around my heart. I literally saw a wall, and on the other side was Jesus wanting so desperately for me to let Him in. I cried. I was so scared! I thought, "What if I get hurt? What if I can't trust You to be who You say You are?" He said, "We will do this only as fast as you are willing; I will never take you where you are not willing to go." I sighed as I removed the first block in the wall - the one in front of my eyes. When I did this I saw His eyes. As I gazed into His eyes I felt a peace and trust come over me. I then felt I could remove a few more blocks, enough to allow His arms to reach over the wall and embrace me. After a few minutes, all that was left of the wall was rubble! I was in my Father's arms…and I felt safe.

He showed me that with time, and as I would allow Him, He would tear down all the walls of self-protection I had erected. I had been going to church and putting on a fake face. When people asked me how I was doing, deep inside I felt they didn't really care, so I would say "I'm doing fine." …I was dying inside.

This is the very tactic the enemy continues to use to keep us isolated and in pain. The enemy tries to convince us that if we share our pain with someone else we will begin to cry - and we don't want to cry or appear weak. The enemy encourages us to think "I don't want to bother them with this" or my favorite, "They will think I'm not a very good Christian."

This is why we must know our identity is in Christ! Otherwise, the enemy of our mind will play games of deception to keep us in bondage. Why wouldn't he want a Christian to function in a false identity? To keep a Christian in bondage to their false identity is to paralyze them from moving forward in their kingdom purposes.

**Mask of Self-Protection**

One of the masks we wear is self-protection. We have been so hurt by others in our lives. We may have even made a vow, something like, "I will never allow myself to be hurt like that again." This doesn't allow us to trust others, and it gives us no room to trust in the Lord. If others get in our bad graces, we cut them out of our lives. Or we may break off a relationship or reject others before they get the chance to reject us. This keeps everyone at a distance to the point that no one has access to the real person - so no one can hurt us.

**Mask of Self-Righteousness (This is religious pride!)**

This mask is a mask of superiority. We like that others need us. We would rather give council to others than look in the mirror at our image. We don't like it when others point out our wrongs, and we judge others' spiritual maturity against our own. We may put ourselves in places and positions in the church to hide behind a title. We rule over others rather than serve them.

## Mask of Self-Reliance

When this mask is worn, you hate to have others help you. You need to be the one helping others. It is an attitude of "I can do it myself" or "I don't need anyone else". This stems from deep hurts that have put you in a place of independence rather than dependence on God.

These are just some of the masks that I was wearing. One by one, as the Lord showed me my masks, I began to hate these things about myself. And that was when I knew that, because I hated the very thing Christ hated, I was ready to hand them over to Him and get rid of them - forever. "Be sincere in your love for others. Hate everything that is evil and hold tight to everything that is good." Romans 12:9 (CEV)

## The Road to Damascus

Sometimes we are like Paul and we need a "Damascus experience" to shine a light on the very things that are keeping us in the dark. It is His kindness that leads us to repentance. Like Paul, many of us hide behind a religious mask that hides our true self. Only when we allow the Lord to truly search our hearts and be open to Him can He begin to deal with the false masks we hide behind, so that our true identity can surface. That night as I wept before the Lord and repented of the masks as He revealed them to me one by one, I began to see my true face emerge. I was scared. I didn't know what to expect. These were my security blankets. I found comfort in those places where I

117

could hide from others and from the pain; by exposing them I would feel naked and vulnerable. But the Lord was there with me and He made a safe place for me to be vulnerable.

**Read Acts 9 and answer the following questions:**

1.   What did Paul do to the Christians before he met Jesus?

_____

2.   Who else heard the voice of Jesus?

_____

_____

3.   What did Paul lose when he encountered the Lord?

_____

_____

4.   Who did Jesus send to Paul?

_____

_____

5.   In v.15, God tells Paul's future job description to Ananias – what is it?

_____

_____

6.   How was Paul healed?

_____

7.    In v. 19, from whom did Paul begin to receive his training? For how long?

_____

_____

8.    How much time passed before they were plotting to kill Paul?

_____

_____

9.    Who protected Paul and helped him to escape?

_____

_____

10.    As we study Paul's life, what masks was he hiding behind before He encountered Jesus?

_____

_____

### *In-to- Me- He- Sees; The Journey Inward- Removing our Masks*

Now it's time for you to ask the Holy Spirit to show you any masks you have been hiding behind. Be bold! This assignment is crucial. Ask the Lord, "What are my masks? Am I hiding behind religious activity? Am I hiding behind self-sufficiency?" You may want to ask this question to trusted friends who you know will speak the truth in love. If you have a mentor, ask him or her to pray with you about these issues. If you are doing this in a group and are bold enough, ask the group. Often, we can't see the masks we are wearing because we have grown comfortable wearing them and seeing ourselves through them. We need trusted people in our lives to point them out to us.

*Dear Father,*

*You are omniscient (all knowing). There isn't a hair on my head that You don't know about. You know my rising up and my sitting down; there is nothing about me You don't already know. You know my past and my future. Knowing this, I can no longer hide from You. Please reveal my masks and my insecurities. Place me in Your cocoon of love and transform my character and soul so that You can be glorified. I choose to hide from You no longer. Forgive me for the false identity I have portrayed. I was only deceiving myself. Forgive me for giving the enemy access to this area of my life. I give it all to You. Forgive me for hiding behind religiosity. Take me to that place where I can trust You completely as You unmask me. In Jesus' Precious Name, Amen.*

Begin to journal what the Lord is showing you about the masks you are wearing and hiding:

_____

_____

_____

_____

_____

_____

_____

_____

_____

_____

_____

_____

_____

_____

_____

_____

_____

_____

_____

_____

_____

**Bonding with the Father: He is Omniscient (all knowing)**
- ❖ **Psalm 44:21**
- ❖ **Psalm 139:1-6**
- ❖ **Matthew 6:8**
- ❖ **Romans 11:33-34**
- ❖ **Colossians 2-3**

**Memorize:**

_"How precious also are Your thoughts to me, O God! How great is the sum of them!"  Psalm 139:17_ (NKJV)

# Lesson 12 - Favor with the King

*"And the king loved Esther more than all the women, and*
*she won grace and favor in his sight more than all the*
*virgins, so that he set the royal crown on her head and made*
*her queen instead of Vashti."*
*Esther 2:17*

We tend to look at the book of Esther from a historical
perspective. As you read and work through this chapter, I
hope that you will begin to understand the story of Esther in
a new way. I hope you will be able to imagine yourself in the
role of Queen Esther and the Lord Jesus as the King. Pay
special attention to the carefully planned process Esther had
to go through to obtain favor with the King.

*Esther 2:12 "Each young woman's turn came to go in to King*
*Ahasuerus after she had completed twelve months'*
*preparation, according to the regulations for the women, for*
*thus were the days of their preparation apportioned: six*
*months with oil of myrrh, and six months with perfumes and*
*preparations for beautifying women."* (NKJV) [emphasis
added]

Esther went through twelve months of preparation - six
months of myrrh treatments and six months of beauty
treatments. Myrrh in this form was an lightly perfumed
yellow-brown oil. The preparation was a purification process;
in Hebrews, the word for this "purification", means
consecration.[3] The process itself was one in which the skin

was scraped. Historically this process of preparation was one that brought humiliation.

All the chosen ladies had to stand naked over a steaming bowl of hot water to open their pores and remove toxins from their bodies. Then their skin would be scraped with a rough brush, and the myrrh would be rubbed all over their bodies - every day for six months.

Notice how six months were spent cleaning out the body and then six months were spent bringing beauty to the outward appearance. The Lord always works from the inside out. He desires a vessel that is completely emptied of self in order to fill it with Him. In becoming all that our King desires of us, we must go through a process that brings death to our desires and wants in order to be completely surrendered to Him. Once we have surrendered, a transformation begins to take place within our hearts so that when we come before the King we will find favor.

It is presumptuous of us to think that we have access to come before the Lord and King without first finding favor in His sight. In Esther's time, to come before the king before you had been invited would have meant death. But if you came into the king's presence and he extended the scepter to you, you knew you had found favor with him. Note how the king responds to Esther when he asks, "What is your request? It shall be given you, up to half of the kingdom." Esther 5:3 (AMP)

A new queen had to be selected because when Queen Vashti was summoned to come before the king she disobeyed and refused to appear. The king could not have a bride that was disobedient to his lordship. Our Lord is also looking for a bride who is willing to come and answer His call. He is looking for a bride that will submit herself to His refining process to become all that she is meant to be.

We are in the place where our King is calling us to submit to the refining process, so that when we come before Him we will find such favor that whatever we ask, it will be given to us.

**Read chapters 1 & 2 of the book of Esther and answer the following questions:**

1.    How long did the feast last?

_____

2.    What was to be done with Queen Vashti because she did not obey the command of the king?

_____

3.    If the King of Kings was calling you to come into His presence so that His glory could be manifested to others, do you think you would answer? _____ Why or why not?

_____

_____

4.    Who took care of Esther when her parents died? (ch. 2)

_____

5.    How many months of treatment did Esther have to endure?

_____

6.    What was the name of the oil that was part of the beautification?

_____

### *In-To-Me-He-Sees; Applying the Myrrh to Our Hearts*

Because of Esther's obedience and submission to the Lord she found favor with the King as well as with man. Much was given to her to prepare her as the new bride of the King, including the oil of myrrh. As we read earlier, the process was one of consecration. Myrrh was often used to prepare bodies for burial. The wise men prophetically gave it to Jesus at His birth (Matthew 2:11), and at His death it was used as a preparation for the body (John 19:39).

Jesus was even offered myrrh mixed with wine when he hung on the cross (Mark 15:23).

### Practicing His Presence

Scripture commands us to crucify our flesh with its lusts and passions. Take time to come into His presence with worship and thanksgiving. Then, when you are ready, pray this prayer and ask the Lord the two questions that follow; write down what He says to you.

*Precious Father, I recognize I need You. I know that You have been trying to show me areas of my life and character I need to submit to You and I have been resisting and complaining. Father, I ask now that You begin to apply the blood judgment of Christ onto the roots of everything that is displeasing to You. I ask for a spirit of revelation to come upon me and show me any areas of my life upon which You would like to apply the oil of myrrh. In Jesus' Name, Amen.*

1. Have I rebelled when I heard the Lord calling me into His presence?

2. What in my heart still needs to have the "Oil of Myrrh" applied to it?

_____

_____

_____

_____

_____

_____

_____

_____

_____

_____

_____

_____

_____

_____

_____

_____

_____

_____

_____

_____

_____

_____

_____

_____

_____

_____

_____

**Bonding with the Father – He is my King**
❖ **1 Timothy 1:17**
❖ **Psalm 145**
❖ **Revelation 19:11, 16**
❖ **1 Timothy 6:15-16**

**Memorize:**

*"The king loved Esther more than all the women, and she won grace and favor in his sight more than all the virgins, so that he set the royal crown on her head and made her queen instead of Vashti." Esther 2:17*

# Chapter 5

# His Healing Presence

# Lesson 13 - Living in the Secret Place

*"He who dwells in the secret place of the Most High shall abide under the shadow of the Almighty."*
*Psalm 19:1 (NKJV)*

During a mission trip to Guatemala in 2006, I began to understand what it truly means to "dwell in the secret place of the Most High." The word "dwell" in this scripture means "to live, a place of habitation."[1] The Lord tells us that if we dwell, or make our place of habitation, in the secret place of the Most High we will be able to remain under the shadow of the Almighty. This secret place is also referenced in Matthew 6:6 *"But you, when you pray, go into your room, and when you have shut your door, pray to your Father who is in the **secret place**; and your Father who sees in secret will reward you openly."* (NKJV) [emphasis added] Your Father is in the secret place waiting for you - behind closed doors!

Only God the Father can speak forth a child's identity. *"I have manifested Your Name [I have revealed Your very Self, Your real Self] to the people whom You have given Me out of the world."* (John 17:6) (AMPC) [emphasis added]. When Jesus came, He introduced us to God as our Father, so that we could understand and walk in the fullness of our identity. If we cannot recognize our purposes and identity, we cannot fully function in our callings. This principle applies to a church or a city, as well as to an individual; without understanding its purpose and identity, any entity fails to achieve its calling.

131

Acts 17:28 says, *"For in Him we live and move and have our being; as even some of your [own] poets have said, for we are also His offspring."* (AMPC) In order to fully live we need to fully understand the Fatherhood of God. The way to do this is to learn to live in the secret place with Him - a place of intimacy. When you were a child, the most cherished times you spent with your parents were probably those you spent together talking and enjoying each other's company. It is the same with our Heavenly Father. He wants to spend time with you in the secret place. He wants you to know Him as your Heavenly Father. The secret place is where you live in His presence continually, not coming and going through times of prayer. This is a place of knowing that He is with you, in you, beside you and behind you at all times. When we make this place our home we find security, purpose, and safety. Psalm 91:4a says, "under his wings you will find refuge". Just as a mother bird places her wings over her baby chicks to protect them, so the Lord covers those who choose to remain near Him. When you are in His Presence, it is as if you are under His shadow of protection. This is what a Father does: He protects you.

Unfortunately, we live in a fallen world where this is not always the case; many of us have been deeply wounded by other people, even our fathers who are supposed to protect us. These wounded feelings often transfer into our relationship with our Heavenly Father. The more you can forgive, the more room you will have in your heart for God's protecting love. If you have ever heard the term "secret place" sometime in your past and this brings up painful memories, remember that God's secret place is one of total protection and safety. A "secret place" that causes pain is a distortion of what God has designed for you.

## Abiding in His Presence

Scripture says the secret place is where we go to meet the Father and talk with Him. Jesus would often go to an isolated area to get away and be with His Father. He had a yearning to stay connected with His Abba. He had lived with His Father for all eternity and yet was willing to leave His Abba for a time so that we would be able to know God the Father as Jesus knows Him. Jesus never struggled with His purpose or identity. When confronted He took authority over Satan which He could do because He learned to remain in the presence of His Father. Jesus was so completely in God's Presence that it was as if they were never separated.

## The Secret Place

Read Matthew 6 and discover how Jesus taught the disciples to communicate with His Father.

1.    When we do good deeds, how are they to be done?

_____

2.    When you pray, how and where are you to pray?

_____

_____

3.    When you pray in secret, how will you be rewarded?

_____

_____

4.   Jesus told His disciples to pray "like this" to teach them that they didn't need a great volume of words to pray effectively. Read v. 9-13 again.

How do each of these relate to you?

v. 9_____

v. 10_____

v. 11 What do you truly need every day?

_____

v. 12 What do you need to be forgiven of and whom do you need to forgive?

_____

_____

### *IN-TO-ME-HE-SEES*

Now that you are done reading the passage, ask the Father to show you what it is that is keeping you from being in the secret place of His Presence. Ask Him to put His finger on those things in your heart that are keeping you from entering into the secret place. Ask Him if there is anyone you need to forgive. If He brings up a memory, or a name, make sure you deal with it. Take some time and write these things out in your journal. Give Him permission to do heart surgery in you! Depend on the revelation of the Holy Spirit and not on the natural mind. Then pray the following prayer to get rid of the obstacles:

*Dear Heavenly Father,*

*Thank You for showing me the damaged areas of my heart that are keeping me from being in the secret place of Your presence. Right now, I confess these as sin. (Name each hindrance). Father I want to abide in the secret place with You under the shadow of your wings. Please forgive me for {name the sin}. And help me to forgive {name the person}. I choose to walk away from these things now in the name of the Lord Jesus Christ and walk into the secret place of Your presence. Thank you, Jesus for showing me the way. Please continually keep me empty of anything but You and Your Holy Spirit. It is through His Blood I pray. Amen.*

**Journal your time with the Lord, what you learned and what you are hearing:**

_____

_____

_____

_____

_____

_____

_____

_____

_____

_____

_____

_____

_____

_____

_____

_____

_____

_____

_____

_____

_____

_____

_____

_____

_____

**Bonding with the Father: He is the Most High**
- ❖  **2 Samuel 22**
- ❖  **Psalm 9:1-2**
- ❖  **Psalm 46**
- ❖  **Psalm 91**
- ❖  **Acts 7:48-50**

**Memorize:**

*"He who dwells in the secret place of the Most High shall abide under the shadow of the Almighty." Psalm 91:1-2* (NKJV)

# Lesson 14 - Removing the False Labels

*"God is spirit, and those who worship Him must worship in spirit and truth."*
*John 4:24*

We live in a society that loves labels. Watch the Emmy awards and you will hear the interviewer ask the star, "So <u>who</u> are you wearing?" We love our labels! I remember as a teenager that not wearing a certain brand name made you "not cool." And when my daughters were teenagers it was the same thing.

There are good labels and bad labels. Do you know you can actually be wearing a bad label spiritually? These are negative labels you give yourself, or others give you, which you receive and wear in your spirit and which begin to impress upon your identity. Those with positions of authority, such as parents, grandparents, teacher, etc. often place these labels, knowingly or unknowingly. They can be related to race, ethnicity, gender, stature, appearance, behavior, etc. We can begin receiving these labels when we are in the womb, as false expectations can be put upon us even at this early juncture in life. A young infant in the womb can begin to carry the false burden of being something that God never intended. You have heard the old saying, "you are what you eat." I contend that we become what we hear.

That is how it was for the woman at the well (John 4:5-30). Here is a woman who had to come out to a public place at a time when no one else would be around. The town had labeled her because of her many sexual indiscretions. Socially she had many strikes against her - being a woman and a Samaritan. (The Jews and the Samaritans greatly disliked each other.) Put yourself in her place; or maybe you have already been there; or maybe you are in this situation currently. Perhaps when you were in school you were the one that everyone picked on and called names. Can you imagine the tears of sadness, hurt and frustration she shed? All she wanted was to be loved. She was searching...thinking perhaps this man...or that man...would meet the deepest needs in her soul. Imagine her surprise to see Jesus at the well! He is there at the very time she is there -when there is usually no one around–a time when she goes to draw water to avoid the townspeople's humiliating taunts. Imagine her thoughts! "What is this man...a Jewish man at that ...doing here at the well? Surely, he must have made a wrong turn! Well...it doesn't matter...he is a Jew, so I know he won't even want to talk to me. He will ignore me, so I can ignore him."

Then, Jesus starts a conversation with her by asking for a drink. Now she is completely caught off guard. He challenges her that if she really knew the gift of God and knew who it was that was asking her for a drink, she would ask for the living water. Can you imagine her thoughts? "Wait a minute. You ask me for a drink and then you want *me* to ask you for living water? When you don't even have anything to draw water with?"

As the conversation progresses, He gently begins to uncover her heart. He has seen all her pain; He was there when she was on her bed crying tears of pain, loneliness, and sorrow. She just wanted to be loved and thought she had to give love in a certain way to receive it. Suddenly, she is face to face with true love! In an instant, He turns her inside out and changes her whole thought process, from a religious mindset to one of relationship, from a false love and seeking after a flawed image of security to a sense of being loved and being safe. One by one, He begins changing not only the labels she has put on herself but also those the community has put on her. When she recognized her inability to live without the True Christ, she willingly died to her old self. She was already dead in her soul, but when Jesus showed up, He brought life. When she left His presence I truly believe there was such a change in her countenance (appearance) that when she began telling others about Christ, they saw the manifest presence of Christ in her. Jesus called into existence this woman's sense of being and brought life from a dead soul. The change was so profound that she was no longer ashamed to declare her newly found love. I don't know about you, but if someone of such reputation came up to me and declared that Jesus the Christ had appeared to her, I don't know that I would believe her. There must have been a powerful change manifested through her because something the townspeople saw in her and heard in her words drew them to come to meet Jesus.

This is the power of a face-to-face encounter with the Living God. He turns us inside out and upside down so that our religious ways of coming to Him are not sufficient. We must worship Him in spirit and in truth. This is a command, not an option. This is what being in Christ's Presence can bring: total transformation.

## Transformation

Just as a butterfly is transformed in the chrysalis, so a person can be transformed in Christ's Presence. When I started my journey into His Healing Presence, the Lord showed me the metamorphic process of a caterpillar into a butterfly. In my mind's eye, He showed me a picture of a caterpillar crawling along a stem. Then it stopped and started building a cocoon. I watched as the caterpillar finished closing itself inside. When I asked the Lord what this was all about, He said, "I am placing you in a cocoon for a while. I am going to transform you from the inside out and when it's time you will emerge a beautiful butterfly."

So many times we grow up with labels that others have put on us, and we wear these labels like old rags. We can't seem to shake them; they become our identity. But they are not the identity the Lord wants us to have. He wants us to take on His identity because we were created in His likeness.

Some of us wear a label of "wife" or "mother" or "daughter", and these are acceptable as long as they are not our identity. Some of us wear labels like "stupid", "dumb", "lazy", "worthless", "clumsy"…the list can go on and on. In an effort to reject these negative labels, we create an artificial persona based on what we want others to think about us. We try to hide our true selves for fear of being rejected or acquiring more negative labels. In reality, we are **not** hiding who we are from the Lord. We can't hide anything from Him; He knows us because He created us. When we enter His Healing Presence He begins to take off these false labels and gives us new labels: "Precious Child" and "Chosen".

## Removing the Labels

In John 4, Jesus went to Samaria to meet the woman at the well. This woman purposely came out in the middle of the afternoon when no one else would be there so she didn't have to face the ridicule of the town. She lived in shame and guilt. When confronted by Jesus she began a transformation right there at the well that caused all her false identities to fall away and a new identity in Christ to take shape. After receiving true revelation of who Jesus was, she was transformed by the truth in her inner being.

**Read John 4:5-30 and answer the questions below:**

1.  According to the scripture, what time of day did the woman come to draw water? _____

2.  The first hour of the day is considered 6 a.m. (dawn); to what time does your answer in #1 correspond?

_____

3.  Where were the disciples at this time?

_____

4.  Why was she surprised that Jesus asked her for a drink?

_____

5.  What is Jesus saying that He can offer the woman if she would believe?

_____

6.    When Jesus asked her about her "husbands", the woman responded that she had how many?

_____

7.    Jesus explained to the Samaritan woman that it is not where she worshipped, but whom she worshipped. How are we to worship Him? In _____ and in

_____.

8.    How could someone with her reputation, who was rejected by the town, proclaim the truth?

_____


_____

## *IN-TO-ME-HE-SEES*

1. Often, it is not only what others say to us but also what we hear and see that cause these negative things to resonate in our souls and pollute our thinking. What we watch on the television, the computer, and in the movies, and what we hear on the radio and in music are major contributors to our lifestyle and alter how we think about ourselves. These influences deeply penetrate our souls in subtle ways; over time they begin to influence our thinking, and eventually our actions. Exposure to inappropriate entertainment is likened to a frog placed in a pot of water that eventually reaches boiling temperature. As the water heats up slowly, the frog becomes desensitized to the heat and incrementally accustomed to the change in the water temperature, never realizing that he is being boiled to death. The same holds true for us; what we

142

would have never watched or listened to in the past, we now learn to tolerate. Ask the Lord to show you ways in which your soul has been defiled through things you have heard and seen. When He reveals something, repent of it and ask Him to take it out of your soul. Ask Him to replace it with His Words and His images. Ask Him to purify your mind and sanctify your imagination.

2. Like the woman at the well we can be wearing false labels. These false labels prevent us from walking in the truth of who we are – in our true identity in Christ. Scripture says "you will know the truth and the truth will set you free" (John 8:32). The chrysalis is the place of rest and discovery of your true sense of being. It is where He shows you the truth of who He is and the truth of who you were meant to be. Tell Him you will allow Him to put you in the chrysalis of His Presence.

*Father, I ask that You bring to remembrance those times when I was falsely labeled. Lord, reveal your truth in each of these instances. Lord, I give You every false label and ask You to show me who I am in You. Amen.*

**Journal what He reveals to you. Ask Him to show you what He does with the labels you give Him.**

_____

_____

_____

_____

_____

_____

_____

_____

_____

_____

_____

_____

_____

_____

_____

_____

_____

_____

_____

_____

**Bonding with the Father – He is Truth**
- ❖ Psalm 51:6; 86:11; 119:160; 145:18
- ❖ John 1:14-17
- ❖ John 14:17; 16:13; 17:17
- ❖ 1 John 1:6-8

## Memorize:

*"God is spirit, and those who worship Him must worship in spirit and truth." John 4:24*

# Lesson 15 - His Healing Words

*"...as it is written, 'I have made you the father of many nations'-in the presence of the God in whom he believed, who gives life to the dead and calls into existence the things that do not exist."*
*Romans 4:17*

When we truly learn how to enter His presence solely for the purpose of being with Him, He begins to transform us. In His Presence is where our true purpose and identity are restored; He calls our purposes into existence. Acts 17:28 says, *"for 'in Him we live and move and have our being'; as even some of your own poets have said, 'For we are indeed His offspring.'"* [emphasis added]

In His presence, all idols are torn down and we begin to see ourselves as He sees us. Our false perception and the false perception from others are torn down. In His Presence life as we know it stops, and He shows us what life should be. In His Presence are rest, peace, joy, and strength.

Only the Sovereign God, our Father, can call into existence the things that do not exist and give life to the dead. He spoke and it happened. With a word and a breath, life was created. Barrenness turns into life. He alone is life; anything outside of Him is death. To be able to function in this world as we are created to requires us coming into His Presence and recognizing our inability to exist without Him.

It is only in His Presence that we find the meaning of true life. He is the only source of life. As we have been studying the scriptures we have been learning that it is in daily relationship with the Lord that He touches our heart. Although Jesus seemed to put His focus on discipling men, there are times you can really see His tender heart as He ministers to women. Jesus knew how to touch the heart of an individual and meet that deep need.

I have discovered that some of us have a hard time believing or receiving compliments when they are given. Others of us, even when we have the loving words of Christ memorized and teach them to others, can't quite believe them in our souls. It is as if there is a blockage between our heads and our hearts. The longest twelve inches is the twelve inches between a person's head and their heart, and unless the Holy Spirit bridges that gap, we will not be able to fully experience the depth of the Love of the Fatherhood of God. This is why many of us don't receive complete healing in our souls: we don't allow ourselves to truly receive His healing words. At some point, we have cut ourselves off from our emotions. We may even, in the midst of our pain, have made a vow to never experience any emotion again. When we shut people out for fear of being hurt we also shut out the Lord. It is only in His incredibly loving presence that we can learn to trust Him. He is the only one who can take away our pain. Only He can meet us at our most vulnerable place and teach us to trust again.

When you come into His presence it is what He says to you that brings about healing. This may be a scripture that comes to mind, an image, or just a feeling that you experience. We have been practicing this all along throughout each lesson. It is my prayer that after this lesson that you will allow the Lord to take you to a new level of listening to His healing words. I pray you will allow His words to wash over the depths of your soul like a balm.

*"For the word of God **is living** and active, sharper than any two-edged sword, piercing to the division of soul and of spirit, of joints and of marrow, and discerning the thoughts and intentions of the heart." Hebrews 4:12* [emphasis added]

The word of the Lord is living; it brings life. It prunes the unhealthy parts of our hearts and souls in so that we might put out roots and grow in faith.

**His Healing Words**

Jesus was invited to dinner by the Pharisees, the religious leaders of the day. During this dinner, a woman came in to tend to Jesus, and, with no thought as to what others might think about her, totally abandoned herself to Jesus in front of the crowd, ultimately pouring the expensive contents of an alabaster jar over Him. I would imagine this made the others there feel uncomfortable, but Jesus never stopped her. She came to minister to Him-asking for nothing and giving her all-expecting nothing, not even a reply. But He stopped and publicly recognized her for her act of love. The Pharisees commented about the words He spoke and criticized Him, but Jesus turned their criticisms back on them and rebuked them. The woman with the alabaster jar literally ministered to Jesus by pouring its contents over Him. She symbolically poured herself out before Him, totally abandoning herself in His Presence. It may seem odd for us to pour out our self so freely, yet she washed Jesus feet. Later, Jesus commanded his disciples to do the same thing for others.

**Read Luke 7:36-50 and answer the following questions.**

As you read these passages about the woman with the alabaster jar pay special attention to the words spoken over her.

1.    What is known about this woman from this passage?

_____

_____


2.    Why was it significant that the Pharisees invited Him to dinner?

_____

_____


3.    What were some of her actions that ministered to Jesus?

_____

_____

_____

_____

_____

_____


4.    In the parable about the two debtors, which person would appreciate it more?

_____

_____

5.    What did Jesus tell the woman after she was done? (v. 48 & 50)

_____

_____

6.    What did Jesus say had healed the woman?

_____

### *IN-TO-ME-HE-SEES*

Today as you spend time in His presence reading the scriptures on the following pages, insert your name into them. Don't let them just be words on a page - apply them to your heart.   Read the Luke passage again, and this time read it aloud. Visualize yourself as the woman with the jar ministering to Jesus. Make this part of your worship. Try to have worship music playing as you do this. Ask Him to speak to you; be still and listen. In the back of the book, I have included additional scriptures entitled "His Healing Love". As an ongoing assignment, each day read one of these verses and apply them to your life. I have left blanks so you can insert your name or a personal pronoun (I, me, etc.). Let the words wash over you and bring healing to your soul.

As you pray the following prayer, place one hand on your head and the other hand over your heart.

*Heavenly Father,*
*I recognize there is a chasm between my head and my heart.*
*I know what Your words say but have yet to truly comprehend*
*their meaning in the depths of my heart.  Please show me what*
*the blockages are.  Please forgive me if I have cut myself off*

*from any of my emotions because of pain I have experienced in the past. Your word says that I can experience the depths of Your love although I may not be able to comprehend it (Ephesians 3:18). Lord, show me any vows I have spoken over my life that have shut down my emotions and made me unable to experience greater depths of Your love.*

**Journal the words you hear so you can hide them in your heart. Pray them as a personal declaration.**

_____

_____

_____

_____

_____

_____

_____

_____

_____

_____

_____

_____

**Bonding with the Father – He is the Word**
- ❖     **John 1:1-2**
- ❖     **John 1:14**
- ❖     **Hebrews 4:12**
- ❖     **Psalm 19:50**
- ❖     **1 Peter 1:24-25**

**Memorize:**

*"And with this Word, God created all things. Nothing was made without the Word. Everything that was created received its life from Him, and His life gave light to everyone." John 1:3-4 (CEV)*

# Chapter 6

# Run to the Cross

# Lesson 16 - Power in the Blood

*"In Him we have redemption (deliverance and salvation) through His blood, the remission (forgiveness) of our offenses (shortcomings and trespasses), in accordance with the riches* and *the generosity of His gracious favor."*
*Ephesians 1:7 (AMPC)*

There are six major weapons of warfare for the healing of our soul: the healing Word(s) of the Lord (previous lesson), the Holy Spirit (two lessons previous), the body of Christ, the cross, the testimony of your Salvation, and the blood of Christ. In this lesson we will discover the power of this blood of Christ to heal us completely.

While we may understand that Christ died, was buried, and rose again on the third day, the whole significance of why His blood had to be shed is often a point of confusion for many people.

The Bible says the blood is Life. This is what the Lord said as He was giving the Israelites specific instructions on how to handle the preparation of animals for eating: "Only be sure that you do not eat the blood, for the blood is the life, and you may not eat the life with the flesh." Deuteronomy 12:23 (AMPC)

The intent was to use the blood for sacrifice; if it were consumed, there would be severe repercussions. "Any one of the house of Israel or of the strangers who dwell temporarily among them who eats any kind of blood, against that person I will set My face and I will cut him off from among his

155

people [that he may not be included in the atonement made for them]. For the life (the animal soul) is in the blood, and I have given it for you upon the altar to make atonement for your souls; for it is the blood that makes atonement, by reason of the life [which it represents]. Therefore, I have said to the Israelites, No person among you shall eat blood, neither shall any stranger who dwells temporarily among you eat blood". Leviticus 17:10-12 (AMP)

The difference comes when you compare the blood of animal sacrifices to the blood of Jesus. Although blood is the life force within us, it is only temporal. The blood of animals was never meant to be the source of eternal life; it was only meant as a payment for specific sins. Jesus alone can be the full atonement for sin. Hebrews 10:4 says, "For it is impossible for the blood of bulls and goats to take away sins." *Webster* defines atonement as "the reconciliation of God and humankind through the sacrificial death of Jesus Christ."[2] The only power the blood had was what the Father alone said it could accomplish. What gave such power to the blood of Christ? It was Christ's offering himself without any sinful stain in His nature or life.

Being flesh, He could have defiled the blood through sin at any time, but because He maintained purity in His body while here on earth, He was able to pay the full price for our sin. The blood of animals covered sin and allowed relationship with God. Jesus' perfect and pure blood brought true intimacy, salvation, and deliverance.

Jesus suffered beatings, humiliation, extreme pain and shed His blood all so that we could be healed.

Isaiah 53:4-5 says, *"Surely He has borne our griefs (sicknesses, weaknesses, and distresses) and carried our sorrows and pains [of punishment], yet we [ignorantly] considered Him stricken, smitten, and afflicted by God [as if with leprosy]. But He was wounded for our transgressions, He was bruised for our guilt* and *iniquities; the chastisement [needful to obtain] peace* and *well-being for us was upon Him, and with the stripes [that wounded] Him we are healed* **and *made whole*."** (AMP) [emphasis added]

He carried our sorrows, pains and bore our punishment. He took on our sickness, weakness, and distress so that we could have physical, spiritual, and emotional healing. His death is what brought salvation. His blood brought healing and deliverance from illness and weaknesses. We are more than healed-we are made whole!

It is His Blood that allows us to have intimacy with the Father. It is His blood that gives life, eternal life, to our carnal bodies. "Indeed, under the law almost everything is purified with blood, and without the shedding of blood there is no forgiveness of sins." (Hebrews 9:22)

There is power in His blood!

**Read Hebrews 9:1-28 & 10:19-23**

1.   Before Christ came, where was the first prepared place of worship? _____

2.   In the Old Testament, what was done before the priest could enter the Holy of Holies?

_____

_____

3.   Christ became the _____ (v. 11) for us by sacrificing His own _____ so that we could enter into the _____ of _____.

4.   Because of His death, we are no longer bound under the first covenant. This enables us to receive our eternal _____.

5.   Sacrifices had to be offered repeatedly in the Old Testament. Jesus only had to pay the price _____ time(s) for all. (v. 28)

6.   We can now enter the holy place through the blood of _____. (v. 19)

## IN-TO-ME-HE-SEES

*"For God, did not send his Son into the world to condemn the world, but in order that the world might be **saved** through him."* (John 3:17) [emphasis added]

The Greek word for saved is *Sozo*, which means, "deliver or protect - heal, preserve, be (make) whole."[3] His blood not only brings healing to our body but it is also meant to bring healing to our soul. Our soul is comprised of our mind, our will and our emotions. Jesus wants to heal the wounds of our hearts and the pain from our past. He suffered rejection and abuse, so He is able to relate to what we have gone through in our lives. Isaiah 53:3 says, *"He was despised and rejected and forsaken by men, a **Man of sorrows and pains, and acquainted with grief and sickness**; and like One from Whom men hide their faces He was despised, and we did not appreciate His worth or have any esteem for Him. Surely, He has **borne our griefs (sicknesses, weaknesses, and distresses) and carried our sorrows and pains [of punishment]**, yet we [ignorantly] considered Him stricken, smitten, and afflicted by God [as if with leprosy]."* (AMP) [emphasis added]

It is time for us to exchange our pain for the joyful life found in Christ. We need a transfusion of His blood which was shed for us. It's time to disconnect from the iniquitous blood line of our past, which can only bring death, and receive a blood transfusion from Jesus, which can bring life. His blood should flow through us to bring life to our hearts, our minds, and our wills. This is what binds us in a new covenant relationship with Him.

With your hand over your heart pray:

*Heavenly Father,*

*You know who I am inside. You know when I cry. You see all my pains and wounds. You know I am in need. I need You, Lord, to apply Your life-giving blood to the wounds of my heart so that my heart will again be able to beat as one that pumps life. Today I choose to receive a blood transfusion from You, to remove all the old, tainted blood and receive fresh, precious blood from Jesus' heart. Please allow Your life's blood to flow through me and bring life to my soul.*

## Journal your time with the Lord

_____

_____

_____

_____

_____

_____

_____

_____

_____

_____

_____

_____

_____

_____

_____

_____

_____

_____

_____

_____

_____

_____

_____

_____

_____

_____

_____

_____

_____

_____

_____

_____

_____

_____

_____

_____

_____

_____

_____

**Bonding with the Father: He is the Source of Life**
- ❖ **Genesis 1:26**
- ❖ **Job 33:4**
- ❖ **John 1:3-5**
- ❖ **Romans 4:17**

**Memorize:**

*"Indeed, under the law almost everything is purified with blood, and without the shedding of blood there is no forgiveness of sins." Hebrews 9:22*

# Lesson 17 - "The Old Rugged Cross"

*"Then Jesus said to His disciples, 'If anyone desires to be My disciple, let him deny himself [disregard, lose sight of, and forget himself and his own interests] and take up his cross and follow Me [cleave steadfastly to Me, conform wholly to My example in living and, if need be, in dying, also].'"*
*Matthew 16:24 (AMPC)*

I love many of the old hymns in which we sing about the cross! They so beautifully depict the price Christ paid for us. The problem is that many of us sing these songs without really paying attention to the words anymore. When the Lord started me on my healing journey, He had me go back to these old hymns, and He convicted me that I wasn't really paying attention to the words. I wasn't allowing them to sink down into the depths of my soul. After I prayed for the healing of my imagination, I found the Lord often placing an image of the cross in my mind. As soon as I would see it in my mind's eye I would immediately go into a deeper level in my worship.

I don't think many of us fully comprehend what Christ went through before He went to the cross and the price He paid while on the cross. The cross was the ultimate form of humiliation. Only the worst criminals (thieves, robbers, murderers, and those who were a threat to the Roman government) were executed this way. This excruciating death was the price they paid for their crimes. Until the release of the movie *The Passion of the Christ*, many people had little insight into the magnitude of suffering on the cross. Some still feel that the torture and bloodshed depicted in the movie were merely "Hollywood as usual", designed to captivate the audience. But every detail of what Jesus went through was the normal procedure for a criminal. When my daughter and I went to see the movie, she remarked upon my lack of reaction to this brutal scene. I explained that I had already experienced the intensity of the price He paid for me through reading the scriptures: Christ having to lie on the rough, rugged cross with open gashes and nails in his hands and feet-His life blood being poured out upon the ground and upon the cross-His blood pouring out from the open wounds as He hung there.

When I teach, I encourage others to use their imagination and visualize the cross before them as they read the scriptures. I also encourage them to picture themselves as one of the people there witnessing the execution, to experience the emotions of those moments. Like the blood of Christ, the cross is a tool that can aid in the healing of our soul. When we approach the cross in our imagination it helps us to forgive others in a deep way. When we view the cross, we see what true forgiveness looks like.

The cross is where grace and mercy met and saved us from eternal death. There are times we need to stop and remind ourselves of the fullness of the price He paid and the price we are supposed to pay. We are not expected to physically die as He did, but there is a death to ourselves that is required. Scripture often talks about being willing to surrender all. This looks different for each of us. Some may be asked to lay down a ministry or a job, others unhealthy relationships. And others may be asked to lay down their reputations. At the same time, the cross also reminds us that death is required to bring about a resurrected life. Whatever the cost, no matter how painful, the reward is always greater.

Abraham knew this all too well. In Genesis 22, the Lord told Abraham he had to lay down his own son's life, his only heir for whom he had waited over 80 years. It was not so much the actions of Abraham that are the key to this story but those of Isaac. Isaac was most probably a young man in his teens at the time, and he was used to going to worship with his father. And as a teenager, he would have been well acquainted with the elements of sacrifice: wood, fire, and a sacrificial animal. As you read the scriptures you see that Abraham bound Isaac's hands and feet. (Genesis 22:9) Binding the hands is symbolic of surrendering that which you put your hands to, i.e. your work, your ministry, how you spend your time. Binding the feet is symbolic of surrendering your ability to go where you please. In order for Abraham to even consider sacrificing his son, Isaac had to be willing; it would be near impossible for an old man to bind the hands and feet of a teenage boy without his cooperation. We do not read in the scriptures that Isaac resisted or argued with his father, but instead we read that he surrendered himself willingly to be sacrificed. Isaac was a prototype of Jesus as portrayed in Matthew 27:2: *"And they bound Him and led Him away and delivered Him over to Pilate the governor."* [emphasis added]

We don't realize the hardship that Jesus endured in surrendering Himself to the cross. Jesus was fully human as well as fully divine. He, like Isaac, was flesh, as we all are. Yet Jesus surrendered and was obedient to His Father. The obedience of Isaac and Abraham was very personal and sacrificial worship to the Lord. As you read the scriptures below you will see that their implements of worship were the wood, the knife, and the fire. Jesus said, "Greater love has no man than this, than to lay down one's life for his friends." (John 15:13) (NKJV) He also says we are to lay down our lives-our agendas and our wills-just as He did.

**Read Genesis 22:1-17**

1.    Who was it that tested Abraham? _____

2.    What was being tested? _____

3.    What did Abraham say he and Isaac were going up to the mountain to do? _____

4.    Who were they going to worship there? _____

5.    What were the three elements of worship he took with them? _____

6.    What did Abraham do to prepare Isaac to be sacrificed?

_____

_____

7.    What is the significance of this substitution for us today? _____

_____

8.    What did Abraham rename the place? _____

9.     How did God say He would bless Abraham because of his obedience? _____

_____

### IN-TO-ME-HE-SEES

There are things the Lord is requiring us to lay down in order to be more obedient to His Will. Let's take time to seek the Lord and see what it is He is requiring of you. This could be a habit, a hobby, the hours you work, your control, your fear...only the Lord knows what He is requiring of you. Are you willing to lay it down for Him?

Pray this in your own words:

*Heavenly Father,*

*I choose to lay down my life as You laid down Your life for me. I ask You, Father, to show me anything that stands in the way of my surrendering my life to You. Please show me what I need to bring to the cross. Lord, not my will but Your will be done. I know that You can provide whatever I need and that You test Your children to see if there is anything we love more that You. Father show me if there is anything I have put before You in my life.*

**Journal His response back to you:**

_____

_____

_____

_____

_____

_____

_____

_____

_____

_____

_____

_____

_____

_____

_____

_____

_____

_____

_____

_____

**Bonding with the Father: The Lord Will Provide (Jehovah Jireh)**
- ❖ **Genesis 22:8, 13-14**
- ❖ **Acts 14:17**
- ❖ **Philippians 4:19**
- ❖ **1 Timothy 6:17**

**Memorize:**

*"I have been crucified with Christ [in Him I have shared His crucifixion]; it is no longer I who live, but Christ (the Messiah) lives in me; and the life I now live in the body I live by faith in (by adherence to and reliance on and complete trust in) the Son of God, who loved me and gave Himself up for me." Galatians 2:20 (AMPC)*

# Lesson 18 - From Curse to Blessing

*"Out of the same mouth proceed blessing and cursing. My brethren, these things ought not to be so."*
*James 3:10 (NKJV)*

In today's society, it is easy to be very negative about life. Increasingly there seem to be people struggling with depression or other forms of mental illness which make it difficult for them to even function day-to-day. But sometimes I wonder…how many are suffering from depression because they have spoken negatively about themselves or have been spoken to in a negative manner since they were young?

I used to be a person who allowed my fears to rule over me. I was an extremely negative, querulous person who never saw the good in anything, only the bad. When I came to know the Lord it was not only hard for me to believe and trust Him but to worship Him, even though I knew worship might be the very thing that could set me free.

I never realized just how much power there was in our words until I read Derek Prince's book *Blessing or Curse, You Choose*. When we use negative words we can speak death instead of life into situations and circumstances in our lives. We were created for communication with our God. Our words, whether negative or positive, are like spoken prayers and have power behind them. Let me give you an example. Several months before I was saved, I was sitting in a hospital waiting room while my mother had back surgery, an 8-hour procedure. I was 19 years old, pregnant, unmarried, and full of fear about my future. Left in the waiting room so long with very little to do, my mind began to wander. Another woman in the room, who was anxiously waiting for her relative to come out of surgery as well, said, "I just want to let you all know that I was recently diagnosed as an epileptic and I have seizures. Because this illness isn't well known, many people don't know what to do if they see someone having a seizure. Anxiety can bring on a seizure, so I wanted to let you know how to handle a seizure if that should happen."

As an already anxious, young mother-to-be, I began thinking, "Lord! (keep in mind I didn't know the Lord Jesus at this time) I would rather pop a pill every day (to control epilepsy) than have to worry about getting cancer." Four months later I had my first seizure. Seven months after that I became a Christian. Then one day I read in the scriptures that God healed an epileptic and so I claimed promises of my healing in the Lord. Twelve years later, I read Derek Prince's book; three months after that we had a gentleman come to our church who was supposed to speak on prayer but instead spoke on the power of the tongue-blessings and curses. I went up to him afterward and shared with him the curse I felt I had on my life. He agreed and prayed with me to break it. Now mind you, I had been before the elders of my church several times seeking healing. But this wasn't a physical healing as much as it was a spiritual healing which manifested itself in a physical way. This gentleman led me in a prayer to break the curse in the same way in which I had prayed from Derek Prince's book three months previously. However, this time I could receive it without any doubt and the prayer was spoken before witnesses. As of April 23, 1996, I have been seizure free! I hope you don't have to learn your lesson the hard way like I did!

God used this instance in my life to reveal my negativity and illustrate how we are to be speakers of life and not death. For the next several weeks He showed me the power of my tongue. I began to realize just how many times a day I spoke curses such as, "that was stupid of me", "you idiot", "I'm sick and tired of….", or "I'm so forgetful." If I spoke or thought negatively, the Holy Spirit would convict me. I would repent and then say aloud, or think, a hopeful and encouraging thought, a blessing. My own words brought a lot of bad things into my life, but I believe the Lord allowed them to show me that there is power in our tongues.

Proverbs 26:2 says, "Like a flitting sparrow, like a flying swallow, So a curse without cause shall not alight." (NKJV)

Why do some curses stick and others don't? It depends on if you have given it cause. Someone that is dear to me took care of her ailing mother who had developed Parkinson's disease near the end of her life. I often heard this woman speak of her concern that she too would develop this disease and suffer like her mother did. A few years after her mother died my dear friend was diagnosed with Parkinson's disease. Job 3:25 states, "For the thing I greatly feared has come upon me, and what I dreaded has happened to me." (NKJV). Fear is one of the doorways that give the enemy access to our lives. Fear gives access for curses to enter and remain in our soul (mind, will, and emotion). I sometimes wonder why so many young people seem to be getting cancer; could it be that their fear of getting the disease gives the enemy access to their health?

## Moving into Blessing

It is my prayer that you will not be fearful as you read this lesson. The enemy only has access because we have given it to him. I pray that you will begin asking the Lord if you have indeed given the enemy any open doors that have allowed curses into your life. As you are cleansed and close these access doors into your life, you will then have the authority to go into battle for your family. You can be the initiator through which the doors to your family can be sealed. It's time to close the doors and deny the enemy access to yourself and your family. It's time to move from curses to blessings! Ephesians 4:29 says, "Let no corrupting talk come out of your mouths, but only such as is good for building up, as fits the occasion, that it may give grace to those who hear."

Those of the Jewish faith have a wonderful history and tradition concerning blessings. They have learned the power of blessing their children, seeding good things into their lives and their futures. They have learned the power of blessing their children to greatness. We, as the Church and as a culture, are generally very negative. But our Father is not negative! He is not a "glass half empty" God. We forget that He is our anchor of hope and He is life. He came to conquer death on the cross so that we could have abundant life. We are our own worst enemy. We forget that, as children of God, we walk in power and authority. If we can't begin to realize the power that is in the tongue how can we recognize and walk in the anointing of the power of the Lord? We must learn to bless and not curse ourselves or others. We need to learn to see things from God's perspective. For instance, when we curse our appearance, we are cursing God's creation. The enemy wants us to curse ourselves because it keeps us in bondage and prevents us from coming into the full purposes of God's plans for us. It's a choice.

**Read James 3**

1. The tongue is likened to (v. 4-5) _____

2. James compares our mouths to two other objects that help guide - what are they? _____

3. James says the tongue has the ability to stain or defile the _____ and set on fire the entire course of _____.

4. We are supposed to bless (whom) _____ with our tongue and yet we tend to curse those who are made in God's _____.

5. Jesus said in Matthew 15:18 *"But what comes out of the mouth proceeds from the heart, and this defiles a person."* According to v. 14 what are the things in our lives that can cause a person to speak so negatively?

_____

_____

6. Where does true wisdom comes from? v. 15 _____

## IN-TO-ME-HE–SEES

It's time to break free from the harsh words spoken by other people and those you inflicted upon yourself. It's time to become a conduit of His Words and Presence. It's time to speak His abundant life into yourself and into those around you, just as Jesus spoke life into all His followers, and continues to speak to us today.

On a separate piece of paper, or on a blank page at the end of this lesson, write down any curses the Lord brings to your mind. Be still and be patient! Ask the Lord to show you the access points (such as fear, shame, anxiety, self-hatred, anger, or unforgiveness). Confess these to the Lord and repent. When you are finished, take time to do this thoroughly, in your own words pray a similar prayer like the one below aloud.

*Heavenly Father,*

*Thank you for revealing to me the power of my words. I confess that I have not used my mouth to bring You glory. I have used it to produce curses. Please show me what curses I have spoken over myself and over other people. Show me any curses I have believed that others have spoken over me.*

*Please forgive me for agreeing with the words of the enemy and speaking out his lies. Forgive me for the access points of _____ that have opened these doors. I choose to forgive _____ for the word curses they have spoken over me. I choose to forgive myself for the curses I have spoke over myself and others.*

174

*Father, In the powerful name of Jesus and through His blood I break off the curse of_____ that is over my life and my family. I evict every demonic spirit (if you have discernment, name the spirit) associated with this curse in the name of Jesus. I now close the access door to this and all demonic spirits and I pray for the infilling of the Holy Spirit. Amen.*

Journal what you believe the Lord is saying to you. Take time to worship and saturate your soul with His presence.

_____

_____

_____

_____

_____

_____

_____

_____

_____

_____

_____

_____

_____

_____

_____

_____

_____
_____
_____
_____
_____
_____
_____
_____
_____
_____
_____
_____
_____

**Bonding with the Father: Receive His blessings**
- ❖ **Genesis 49:25**
- ❖ **Deuteronomy 28:2**
- ❖ **Psalm 21:3**
- ❖ **Psalm 122:7**
- ❖ **Ephesians 1:3**

**Memorize:**

*"Not returning evil for evil or reviling for reviling, but on the contrary blessing, knowing that you were called to this, that you may inherit a blessing. For he who would love life and see good days, let him refrain his tongue from evil, and his lips from speaking deceit." 1 Peter 3:9-10 (NKJV)*

# Chapter 7

# A New Heart

# Lesson 19 - Heart Surgery

*"And I will give you a new heart, and a new spirit I will put within you. And I will remove the heart of stone from your flesh and give you a heart of flesh."*
*Ezekiel 36:26*

God is a triune being comprised of the Father, Son, and the Holy Spirit. And because we have been made in His image, we have been created as triune beings as well. 1 Thessalonians 5:23 says, "And the very God of peace sanctify you wholly; and I pray God your whole spirit and soul and body be preserved blameless unto the coming of our Lord Jesus Christ." (NKJV) When we are saved the Holy Spirit comes and resides in our spirit. Our soul consists of our mind, our will, and our emotions. When the Bible talks about the heart it is speaking about the seat of our emotions. In fact, the Bible tells us to "Keep your heart with all diligence; for out of it *spring* the issues of life." (Proverbs 4:23) (NKJV) When we have been hurt by others (physically, verbally, emotionally, or spiritually), our hearts can become hardened. When our spiritual hearts are not functioning as they should because of our wounds, our physical bodies may not function as well as they should either. A hardened spiritual heart is unable to love unconditionally. Depending on the level of hurt experienced, you can become frigid, unkind, and unresponsive to the needs of others. You can often see these emotions on people's faces; they often look older than their years and their faces appear hardened and unsmiling. This hardness of the heart is caused by unforgiveness.

I know we dealt with unforgiveness in a previous chapter, but it bears revisiting. You may feel that you dealt with unforgiveness the first time around and wonder why you should do it again. I remember thinking that very thought. But I now know that this is a powerful stronghold, and it is difficult to remove from our lives. I believe that the Lord wants to take us deeper in forgiveness to increase our healing from pain and hurts.

I love my father. He and my mother did the best they could in raising their children. They both had extremely difficult childhoods of their own. My mother grew up living first with her aunts and uncles and later in a Christian girls' school. My father's parents divorced when he was young, and he lost all contact with his birth father. When he tried to reconnect with his father, he found he no longer had any place in his father's life. The only father he knew and called "Dad" was his stepfather. But his stepfather was in the Air Force; with the constant moving, there was no real stable "father figure" in my dad's life. These kinds of circumstances can shape a child's character at a very young age. The family issues my parents suffered left character flaws and voids in their lives, which, in turn, also produced voids and character flaws in mine. Hurt people hurt other people, however unknowingly or unintentionally.

When I became a parent, I was no better. I grew up struggling with deep anger. Eventually, the Lord began to show me that I was still harboring unforgiveness and that this unforgiveness was affecting the relationships with my entire family, especially my husband and my oldest daughter. Anger now impacted four generations. But most importantly, this anger was keeping me from a deeper relationship with my Heavenly Father.

My parents, like most of us, tried to be better parents than the previous generation. But we don't live in a perfect world. Even our first parents, Adam and Eve, were not perfect; the Fall showed us that. No generation has an example of perfect human parents. Our only perfect example is God the Father.

One of the best ways to determine if you have completely forgiven someone is to be around that person and see if your "old self" surfaces. I learned to gauge the healing of my relationships based on how I responded to those who had once wounded me. My husband became a great support, as I needed help with my attitude; he knew how much I wanted to truly love those who had once hurt me, not just in words but also in deeds. I didn't want my woundedness to get in the way of any relationship. The vicious cycle I had gotten into had to stop, so I made a commitment to the Lord and said that I wanted the anger to stop with me. I desperately wanted healing! I sought out the Lord to heal this wound and to heal my relationships with others. I told Him, "Whatever it takes, Lord, I am willing." It was a journey of death to my hurts and a death to holding onto grudges and anger.

Anger, bitterness, resentment…these things harden our hearts. We can only restore our hearts of flesh if we allow the Lord to give us his Heart. We have to choose to undergo a heart surgery! You may have heard heart patients say that they begin to feel differently almost immediately after a heart transplant, experiencing cravings and feelings they had never had before. How much more would this be true if we receive a heart transplant from the Lord?

## Inner Healing

Inner healing, or healing of the soul, comes when we ask the Lord to get to the root of the hurt and offenses we have with others. Often it is not a one-time offense but many offenses - some deeper than others- that we need to deal with through the help of the Lord. You may have dispensed with one issue but the Lord wants you to look deeper, to other issues buried deep within. When a hurtful memory or feeling surfaces, first test it by asking the Holy Spirit to only bring up truth and to cancel out any lies you may believe about this person or the situation. Remember that some wounds can be based on what we perceived, not a person's intention, so our feelings may not be true. Once the truth is revealed, ask the Lord to show you <u>your</u> part of the sin, such as an inappropriate reaction, unforgiveness, or anger you have harbored.

You may be tempted to stop at this point because you feel the pain again, and this could cause you to withdraw. I want to encourage you to keep pressing in and asking the Lord to show you the truth. He is with you and will not allow you to be harmed in this process. As the Lord shows you, write down the emotions associated with each memory.

Keep in mind that forgiveness is a choice, not a feeling. You probably won't want to forgive, but because Christ has forgiven us, we are required to do the same. When God brings up these issues it is not because he hasn't forgiven you. He just wants you to forgive those who have hurt you and apply the same grace He has poured out on you. He is showing you that, as you forgive, you are releasing that person from any obligation you feel is owed you. This allows God to have further access into your soul. Negative thoughts and feelings that consume or distract you are obstacles in your life to having more of Him.

You may be asking, "What do I do if the person is not alive anymore?" or "What if I can't face the person I have issues with?" The answer is that is does not matter; reconciliation starts and ends with you. If the person is not alive, or you can't face them, you can write a letter to that person, requesting their forgiveness and releasing forgiveness to them. Name the specific offenses, pray, and release the offenses to the Lord.

There are three major "people" we need to remember to forgive when dealing with inner healing: God, our selves, and the offenders. We may not realize it, but we could harbor anger towards God by blaming Him for our wound. Don't skim over this: you don't know until you ask! Forgiving ourselves is often difficult because we can blame ourselves for the situation. For example, I have ministered to many who blame themselves for a rape or molestation. This is one of those lies we must cancel. Of course, like in previous lessons, we must also make our wills forgive the offenders and let Jesus deal with them.

After you acknowledge the emotion attached to the memory, ask the Lord to show you the lie you believed concerning the wound. Then ask Abba to show you His truth that counters the lie.

We then renounce any lies and any demonic spirits attached to the memories (ex: fear, anxiety, anger, rejection, sexual immorality, etc.) as the Lord reveals them.

Do the study below for further understanding of why we must release forgiveness.

**Read Mathew 18:21-35**

1.   How many times are we to forgive? _____

2.   What did Jesus mean when he said "seventy times seven"?

_____

_____


3.   How much did the servant owe his master? _____

4.   How much did the servant owe the king?

_____


5.   How much was owed to the servant by one of the other servants?

_____

_____


6.   Where does the master send the servant because of the servant's unwillingness to release forgiveness?

_____

_____


7.   What does Jesus say Our Heavenly Father will do if we don't release forgiveness to others?

_____

_____

## IN-TO-ME-HE-SEES

Jesus gave an example in scripture about unforgiveness through the parable of the debtor in Matthew. Ephesians 4:26b-27 says, "do not let the sun go down on your anger, and give no opportunity to the devil." Allowing the door of unforgiveness to remain open gives the enemy access to your soul which in turn can form a stronghold of anger. Unforgiveness keeps you spiritually chained to that person forever. As we learned earlier, this can be passed down for generations. Do you see the crazy contradiction in a person who allows someone to control their emotions because they hold them in unforgiveness, yet at the same time they pray, "Lord, I surrender all"?

It is time to clean out the temple of God!

Pray with me in your own words:

*Father, I desire to have whole-hearted devotion to You. I know that parts of my heart are still controlled by anger, bitterness and unforgiveness. I ask that You remind me of anyone I still have failed to forgive completely. I want nothing to come between You and me, including my anger, bitterness, unforgiveness, or other sin of _____ towards _____. Right now, through power of the Blood of Your Son Jesus, I choose to forgive _____ (their name) for _____ (the offense they committed).*

*I ask Your forgiveness for my part in this sin and I pray and release a blessing right now to _____ (name the person(s)). If they don't know you as Lord and Savior, I pray they will come to know You as such very soon.*

185

You may have to spend some time doing this, allowing the Lord to bring up names of more people than you might at first remember. As He brings up these names, go back and pray this prayer for each one. Don't be too quick to rush through this or you might miss what the Lord really wants you to receive. You may even need to go to a prayer partner and allow them to pray with you, asking that God will bring revelation of anyone in your past that you need to forgive. Sometimes we often look for others to blame for our circumstances. For some this may include blaming God. While dealing with unforgiveness, remember to make sure that you deal with any unforgiveness towards yourself, or apologize to the Lord for harboring unforgiveness towards Him.

After you have released forgiveness to everyone and repented of all bitterness, anger, jealousy, rage, and hatred, pray the following prayer with authority:

*In the Name of the Lord Jesus Christ and through His blood, I evict and cut off every spirit of anger, jealousy, bitterness, unforgiveness, hatred and rage. You no longer have legal access to me! Be gone, now!*

*Holy Spirit, I now ask You to come and fill me with love, joy, unity, and peace. I receive more of You. Come and send Your refreshing peace to me.*

You will find as time goes on, that other offenses will occur or more old ones will spring to mind. Be quick to repeat this process of forgiveness, confession, and blessing to continue the cleansing process.

When you're finished, write in your journal what you have experienced and thank God for freeing you from the tormentors.

_____

_____

_____

_____

_____

_____

_____

_____

_____

_____

_____

_____

_____

_____

_____

_____

_____

_____

_____

_____

_____

_____

_____

_____

_____

_____

_____

_____

_____

_____

_____

_____

_____

_____

_____

_____

_____

**Bonding with the Father: He is Merciful**
- ❖ **Exodus 34:6**
- ❖ **2 Chronicles 30:9**
- ❖ **Psalm 116:4-7**
- ❖ **Hebrews 8:13**

**Memorize:**

*"Be angry and do not sin; do not let the sun go down on your anger and give no opportunity to the devil." Ephesians 4:26-27*

# Lesson 20 - Victim or Victor

*"Arise [from the depression and prostration in which circumstances have kept you - rise to a new life]! Shine (be radiant with the glory of the Lord), for your light has come, and the glory of the Lord has risen upon you!"*
*Isaiah 60:1 (AMPC)*

Some of us have been through horrendous experiences in life. My husband and I minister to many who have been victims of some form of abuse. Once a person has been opened spiritually to an abusive situation it can often open the door for more abuse to occur. In a previous lesson, we studied how detrimental it can be to be labeled with negative words. After just one experience of abuse, a person is labeled by others, or perhaps is self-labeled, as a victim. For many, that label can be applied at a very young age and can be carried around all their lives. And for the rest of their lives they seem to attract that form of abuse, and they can't figure out why. The cause for this is the first trauma experience which can open a door to a spirit of perversion, and, subsequently, attracts other spirits of perversion. It is nothing they did, but what was done to them that opened this door. Spiritually speaking, a person can become a magnet for the very thing they despise.

For one person to whom I ministered this started at just four years old when her relative was inappropriately affectionate towards her. This seemed to create a pattern for her so that between the ages of 7 and 21, there were several other incidents where older men would inappropriately touch her. With each touch, she would get angry - angry that she didn't speak out. Then guilt, shame and other lies from the enemy began to creep into her soul and began destroying her self-esteem. It was as if she began wearing an advertisement to these men saying, "Victim here!" For years, she suffered with shame and loneliness; she felt rejected and unloved by everyone in her life. It wasn't until we talked that she realized she was still living as a victim.

## Access points

There are three access points by which the enemy can gain entrance to our souls.

The first access point is our personal sin. We have been dealing with this for several chapters now, but it is a continual process as the Lord brings revelation to the areas He wants to heal within you. It is like peeling an onion, layer after layer, removing one sin after another. Just because we have come to know Christ doesn't mean that all our sin patterns are instantly broken. It takes time, discipline, obedience and perseverance to break these sinful habits in our lives.

Daily we need to take ownership of the sins we have committed and not play "the blame game". It is often easier to blame others or our circumstances, but until we examine all the entry points into our lives by the light of the Holy Spirit, our hearts will not experience full healing. Doors will remain open, allowing the enemy to come in and out as he pleases.

Often we cannot recognize these access points because we are blinded amidst our pain. It takes the help of the Holy Spirit to illuminate the situation so that the sinful root can be exposed and pulled out and the access door closed. Then we can exchange the roots that were hidden in darkness for His glory and truly walk out the verse at the beginning of this lesson.

The second access point is trauma, as in the case of a young child who was molested or a person who was raped. It was the sin of another that has forced an open door into an innocent person. I want to repeat this: they did not sin. They are truly victims, but the enemy wants them to stay in that place of being a victim instead of being victorious. They themselves have done nothing to deserve what has happened, regardless of their age or lifestyle. Although lifestyle can contribute to the victimization if it is not changed, the victimization does not have to continue.

Any time a person goes through a trauma, especially as a child, the soul becomes open as a result of that trauma. It doesn't matter the type of trauma because we all react differently. Unless the door of this access point is recognized and closed, it continues to give access to the enemy. I went through a very difficult trauma when I was a young child. My grandfather lived close by and would often visit. One day while I was at school, his stomach ulcer ruptured. I came home to the aftereffects of that rupture and never saw my grandfather again; he died several days later. For me, as a six-year-old, this trauma gave access to the spirit of fear, specifically the fear of death or dying. It wasn't until recently that I felt victory over these same spirits.

Traumas often produce a memory that can be very painful. In Section I of this book, The Journey Explained, we asked the Lord to heal our eyes not just for the unclean things we look at but also for the evil things we have witnessed. Healing of the trauma helps bring healing to a tormenting memory and is an important step in closing the access door because we no longer live in the pain of the past. We will be discussing more about the healing of memories later in this lesson.

The third access point can come from your family lineage. Exodus 20:5 states, "You shall not bow down yourself to them or serve them; for I the LORD your God am a jealous God, visiting the iniquity of the fathers upon the children to the third and fourth generation of those who hate Me." (Deuteronomy 23:3 says that sexual sins are passed on for 10 generations!) Often when ministering to people who struggle with sexual issues, their struggles can be traced back through the family history. Nowadays, it is difficult to find a family that has not struggled with sexual sin in some way over so many generations. A familiar spirit is a spirit or demon that serves or tempts an individual to fall into the same sin with which a family member struggled. Sin is written into the memory at the point of the offense, and like the color of one's eyes, this is passed on at the time of conception. If you don't know how to close the access point, it can continue to affect you, your children, their children and on to subsequent generations.

When my husband and I started studying healing and deliverance, the Lord revealed not just physical healing but also spiritual healing. I remember hearing news reports that claimed to discover the DNA of alcoholism. Later research claimed to have found a gene related to homosexuality. These finding later proved to be false, but many do believe they were created this way. As I prayed and sought the Lord, He reminded me that when He created mankind, our DNA was pure. Our DNA later became defiled because of sin after The Fall of Man. The enemy cannot create, but he loves to bring deformity to what God has formed. It would be just like him to want to show "scientifically" that our sins are genetic. That way, man can justify his sin by claiming, "I was created like this, so this is who I am" and "I can't help it". If we are born predisposed to certain sins it is because of the fall of man and these familiar spirits that are passed down through our bloodlines because of human sinfulness.

But we serve a God who created the very DNA of man! He created us to bring Him glory. His desire is to bring complete healing to us. It is only in the light of His presence that the lies can be exposed. I believe the Lord allowed these news reports to show us that prayer for healing should include the healing of our DNA so we do not affect future generations. Even if you do not know your family lineage beyond your own life, the Holy Spirit does. He will bring revelation to that which needs to be dealt with through you to bring healing to yourself and your descendants. Since we know sin entered with Adam and Eve, we know we can ask the Lord to restore our DNA all the way back before the time when sin corrupted it. There is no magic formula, only learning to listen to the Holy Spirit to bring revelation.

I believe that the Church will arise in greater anointing and power if only she would truly deal with the hidden sins of sexual perversion. This kind of sin, above all others, seems to be key in holding the Church in bondage because it is easily accessed and done secretly in the privacy of our own homes and workplaces.

**Read 2 Samuel 11:2-5; 12:1-13; 13:1-14 & 1 Kings 11:1-12**

Let us see how sin affected the family lineage of David:

1.    David already had many wives and concubines, but in 2 Samuel, he gave in to his lust for another woman. Who was she? _____

2.    Who did the Lord send to David to lead him to repentance?

_____

3.    Did David repent? _____

4.    What was the consequence of his sin? (2 Samuel 12:11)

_____

_____

5.    What did David's son Absalom do to his sister? (2 Samuel 13:14) _____

6.    Although Solomon also had many wives, he did not commit adultery with another man's wife as David did. But because of his lust for women what sin did he fall into?

_____

_____

7.   What was the consequence of Solomon's sin? (1 Kings 11:11)

_____

_____

8.   Did Solomon repent? _____

### *IN-TO-ME-HE-SEES*

As we read the scriptures about David's life we can see how his sins were passed down and magnified in his offspring. This was caused through inherited sin which I refer to as corrupted DNA. Our Heavenly Father, who knit us together in our mother's womb, is the only one who can restore the original design. He used the Second Adam, Jesus, to show us that mankind is meant to have the incarnate Christ dwelling in us. It was His blueprint to "make man in his own image" (Genesis 1:26). He showed us it is possible to have the fullness of Christ dwelling in us, as made known in Colossians 2:9-10. "For in Him the whole fullness of Deity **(the Godhead) continues to dwell in bodily form** [giving complete expression of the divine nature]. And you are in Him, made full and having come to fullness of life **[in Christ you too are filled with the Godhead--Father, Son and Holy Spirit--and reach full spiritual stature]**. And He is the Head of all rule and authority [of every angelic principality and power]." (AMPC) [emphasis added]

For our DNA to be restored, we must pray and ask the Holy Spirit to expose the roots of every sin within us. Only your Heavenly Father knows where your DNA has become corrupted, leading to a sin disposition or defect. He has

195

supplied the precious blood of His son to kill these roots. Colossians 1:20 states, "And God was pleased for him to make peace by sacrificing **his blood on the cross**, so that all beings in heaven and on earth would be brought back to God. (CEV) [emphasis added]

Let's pray:

*Father, through the Blood of your Son that was shed for me, I ask You to delve into the roots of sin that corrupt my DNA that you will deal, not only with the DNA issues within me, but also within my family and the future generations to come. I apply the blood judgment of Christ onto these DNA root defilements and ask Your Holy Spirit to bring to light any of the sinful character issues that have affected my family lineage.*

Now wait and listen as the Lord reveals these issues, whether it is a hereditary disease or a sin issue. Write them out in the journaling section on the next page.

Once you have your list then begin to repent and cut it from your lineage:

*Father, please forgive me and both sides of my family all the way back to Adam and Eve for (name the sin or disease that was revealed to you). I apply the blood atonement of Christ to this sin and ask You to restore my DNA. In the Name of Jesus, I cut off this sin in my life and in all future generations in my bloodline. Spirit of (name the sin or disease), I command you through the blood of Christ to be gone now in the name of Jesus. You no longer have access. Your assignment has been canceled in Jesus' name. Holy Spirit, come and restore the original design of God the Father to my*

196

*DNA and my family's DNA. Thank you, God, for Your Creative Power bringing healing and wholeness to my whole being.*

Once you have finished, journal what the Lord has said to you and your experiences during this time. Then give thanks to the Lord and worship Him for this revelation and healing!

_____

_____

_____

_____

_____

_____

_____

_____

_____

_____

_____

_____

_____

_____

_____

_____

_____

_____

_____

_____

_____

_____

_____

_____

_____

_____

_____

_____

_____

_____

_____

_____

_____

_____

_____

_____

_____

**Bonding with the Father: He is the Light**

❖　　Psalm 18:28
❖　　Psalm 36:9
❖　　Psalm 43:3
❖　　Psalm 90:8

## Memorize:

*"But if we [really] are living* and *walking in the Light, as He [Himself] is in the Light, we have [true, unbroken] fellowship with one another, and the blood of Jesus* Christ *His Son cleanses (removes) us from all sin* and *guilt [keeps us cleansed from sin in all its forms and manifestations]."*　　*1 John 1: 7 (AMPC)*

# Lesson 21 - The Garden of our Hearts

*"He answered, 'Every plant that my heavenly Father has not planted will be rooted up.'"*
*Matthew 15:13*

Our Heavenly Father planted a garden within each of us when we receive Christ. In this garden planted by His Spirit were seeds meant to produce fruit of love, joy, peace patience, kindness, goodness, faithfulness, gentleness, and self-control (Galatians 5:22-23). But sometimes weeds can also grow in this garden. Anyone who has ever tried planting any seeds knows this. No matter how carefully you prepare, you eventually must either pull up the weeds or put down some kind of weed killer, or both, to keep the weeds out of the garden! Yet many of us don't even realize our hearts are gardens that also need tending. The weeds of sin can come in, and, if not attended to on a regular basis, they cause the beauty of the garden to be destroyed. Genesis 2:15 states, "The LORD God took the man and put him in the garden of Eden to **work it and keep it**." [emphasis added] The word "keep" comes from the Hebrew word *Shawmar*, which means, "to protect, lay wait for, as a watchman would."[1]

Our spiritual hearts are no different; we need to guard the garden of our hearts to keep the enemy from coming in. If Adam had done what God had commanded then maybe the serpent would not have had access to deceive Eve. Notwithstanding, this commandment is to all of us to work and to keep the garden of our hearts. If we don't, then, like Eve, we can be deceived and not even realize we are in the midst of sin. The enemy is not creative; he works to distort the truth by planting opposing seeds of hate, sorrow, struggle, impatience, cruelty, immorality, faithlessness, callousness, and overindulgence. Our role is to remain and abide in Christ so that our fruit can remain. John 15:4 says, "Stay joined to me, and I will stay joined to you. Just as a branch cannot produce fruit unless it stays joined to the vine, you cannot produce fruit unless you stay joined to me" (CEV).

In contrast, if we allow the weeds to come in, they begin to choke the good fruit and make room for the bad fruit. And it starts at the roots. Have you ever noticed the roots of weeds are often stronger than other flowering plants in your garden? Take dandelions: they are tenacious weeds that grow very quickly and have long strong roots that make it very hard to pull them out. If you don't remove the entire root, the dandelion grows right back, and it grows much faster than the other flowering plants! I once had a next-door neighbor whose garden was full of dandelions. The neighbor on the other side would complain to me about it because she was fearful the dandelions would infest her yard as well. She asked me to confront our neighbor with her so that neither of our yards would be infested with the weeds. If only we were half as concerned about the garden of our hearts.

Have you ever noticed when you pull out a root that it has many small, attached offshoots that can grow to form new plants? It is no different with sin. What we think is the root issue of a sin is often just an offshoot of the main root, a symptom, if you prefer, of a bigger core issue. For example, the root of fear is control, and control is rooted in pride. Pride is the main root. It was pride that caused Satan himself to think he was better than God. Ultimately, the main root of every sin is pride. Satan will use the sin of fear to keep us from trusting the Lord.

Fear tempts us to take control of a situation and not allow the Lord to handle it, which takes our eyes from the Lord and weakens our trust in Him. Satan tempted Eve and told her she "would be as God, knowing good and evil" which piqued her pride. Where was Adam? Why was he not watching over the Garden? Instead, he too allowed himself to be tempted.

Scriptures speak a great deal about the heart and how the words we speak reveal the true condition of our hearts. So if we still contend with issues of hatred, anger, or other sins, they will end up eventually being exposed amidst our conversations with others. If we hear bitterness in our voices or feel angry or ashamed when we talk about a person or an incident, this is indicative that we still have root issues that need to be dealt with.

Now that we have begun to receive healing of our hearts we need to guard our hearts from the enemy's return. This was ground we took back, and we need to keep the little foxes out of the garden of our hearts. (See Judges 15:3-5. Little foxes can ruin a whole grain field in no time!)

**Read Matthew 12:31-37; Mark 7:21- 23; Luke 6:41- 46**

1.    According to scripture, how can we tell what is in someone's heart? _____

2.    A good person brings forth _____and evil person brings forth _____

3.  Jesus says by our words we will both _____ and
_____ . (Matthew 12:37)

4.  According to Mark, from where does Jesus say our
thoughts come?

_____

5.  In Luke, Jesus tells the disciples that they cannot take
the speck out of another's eye until they take the _____ out
of their own.

6.  In Luke 6:44 what does Jesus say we are known for?

_____

## IN-TO-ME-HE-SEES

Joel 2:12-13: "Therefore also now, says the Lord, turn and
keep on coming to Me with all your heart, with fasting, with
weeping, and with mourning [until every hindrance is
removed and the broken fellowship is restored]. Rend your
hearts and not your garments, and return to the Lord, your
God, for He is gracious and merciful, slow to anger, and
abounding in loving-kindness; and He revokes His sentence
of evil [when His conditions are met]." (AMPC)

Only the Lord can shine His light on the roots of the sins
within our hearts and expose them. I remember my return
from China in 2006 when the Lord showed me a vision of a
large driller boring a hole in the ground. When I asked Him
what it meant, I saw the drill come out of the hole entangled
in roots. The lord told me He was digging up the deep roots

within my soul, and so I asked Him the name of the roots. He said they were fear and intimidation, which, as I mentioned earlier, are rooted in fear of losing control and, of course, pride. In my case, I was allowing fear of man to intimidate me instead of seeking God and trusting Him to be in control.

As I prayed about these root issues, He gave me this scripture: Ephesians 3:16-19. "That according to the riches of His glory He may grant you to be **strengthened with power through His spirit in your inner being**, so that **Christ may dwell in your hearts** through faith-**that you, being rooted and grounded in love**, may have strength to comprehend with all the saints what is the breadth and length and height and depth, and to know the love of Christ that surpasses knowledge, that **you may be filled with all the fullness of God**." [emphasis added]

The roots had to be pulled out for me to receive the fullness of God. As I prayed this verse, I saw the Lord filling up the hole that was dug with His love, and then I heard Him say, "There is no fear in love; but perfect love casts out fear, because fear involved torment. But he who fears has not been perfected in love." (1 John 4:18) (NKJV)

Now it's your turn. Close your eyes and begin to pray and ask the Lord to show you the garden of your heart. Ask him to show you the beauty of the garden. As He does, take the time to really see the garden of your heart and all that He has planted in you. Now ask Him to show you any weeds in your garden that are choking out the seeds He has planted in you. Ask Him to bring revelation of the names of the weeds in your garden. Now ask Him to help you pull them out and watch what he does. He showed me a huge drilling machine, but in

203

your case, the Master Gardener may have a different approach.

As you deal with these roots, ask the Gardener of your heart to minister to you and plant new seeds of the opposite spirit in their place. If you are having problems killing the roots, you may need the prayer support of others. Don't be afraid to ask for help, especially since this could be a necessary first step for you to kill the root of pride.

Once you have finished, journal all that the Lord has said and shown you and your experienced during this time with the Lord. Then give thanks and worship Him for this revelation. You might want to draw pictures and describe what your garden looks like.

_____

_____

_____

_____

_____

_____

_____

_____

_____

_____

_____

_____

_____

_____

_____

_____

_____

_____

_____

_____

_____

_____

_____

_____

_____

**Bonding with the Father: He is the Gardener**

- ❖ **Genesis 1:11-12**
- ❖ **Matthew 15:13**
- ❖ **Mark 12:1-9**
- ❖ **1 Corinthians 3:6**

**Memorize:**

*"By this my Father is glorified, that you bear much fruit and so prove to be my disciples." John 15:8*

# Section III – The Outward Journey

# Sharing the Journey with Others

# Sharing the Journey with Others

I remember when I first moved to Cleveland, Ohio from Pennsylvania in 1992. I was a young mom of three daughters and had just left the only home I knew, moving from a very rural setting into a suburb of Cleveland. We found the same church denomination -the only one we knew to go to and felt safe in- here in Cleveland. I was excited for a fresh start but realized I was not good at making friends. However, I came to find acceptance through ministering to others in our new church. I was neither very old nor mature in the Lord, but the pastor assumed we knew more than we did, for some reason, and we happily accepted the compliment. We did not recognize the inappropriate speed by which we were placed into positions of ministry. I somehow managed to appear more mature than I really was and more knowledgeable than most people there. I was continually asked to teach, lead activities, or form committees, so it came as a shock to everyone when I heard the Lord say to pull out of everything. I felt I could no longer continue to pretend to be something I was not.

Even the pastor couldn't understand that I, who was always the one ministering to others, needed someone to minister to me. It seemed there was no one in the church who could even understand. It was then that I went into a season of hiding, hiding from others and all church responsibility. I needed to find out who I was in Christ, who I was created to be, and how I was to bring Him glory. As I went through this season (outlined in the middle section of this book, "The Inward Journey") I began to discover who I was. When this season of safety and security ended, emerging again was scary because I was no longer the person others thought they knew. Once again, the requests to be involved in ministry came forth but I turned them down because I had come to realize these no longer fit the person that Christ had created me to be. For a while I filled non-leadership roles in the church, which surprised and seemed to disappoint a lot of people.

I found that my passions began to mesh with the purposes for which God had created me. During that season of being hidden, seeking the Lord, He began pointing out scriptures that underscored my identity, calling out and birthing in me a vision for something I would never have seen while I was so busy with church leadership. The Lord impregnated me with purpose and vision for something He had created beforehand specifically for me. Ephesians 2:10 says, "For we are his workmanship, created in Christ Jesus for good works, which God prepared beforehand, that we should walk in them."

You have a creative purpose. As you read this portion of my story, I pray that the Spirit of God will bring you revelation as to what you are called to be and do that will bring glory to your Heavenly Father. Isaiah 43:21 "This people I have formed for Myself; They shall declare My praise." (NKJV)

# Chapter 8

# Created to BE

# Lesson 22 - Created to Be ...

*"And God blessed them. And God said to them, "Be fruitful and multiply and fill the earth and subdue it and have dominion over the fish of the sea and over the birds of the heavens and over every living thing that moves on the earth."*
*Genesis 1:28*

Over the years, many people have asked, "What is our purpose on earth? For what reasons were we created?" During the journey to find myself, I decided to search the scriptures to see why the Lord created us. What better place to look than at the beginning when the Lord created mankind? After the Lord created Adam and Eve, The Word says He blessed them and said, "Be..." This is a powerful command for life itself. Notice God is saying BE, not DO. Too many of us get caught up in the "doing". Life is not about what we do but that we achieve a state of "being" with God, through God, and in God. We are called to "be fruitful and multiply and fill the earth". He gave the animals the very same blessing earlier in the chapter. (Genesis 1:22) They were to propagate and reproduce. But He adds a further command to Adam and Eve that was not for the animals: they were to subdue the earth and have dominion over every living thing that moves. Dominion is a strong word meaning "to have the power to rule, to exercise control, to have supreme authority, or have sovereignty".[1]

In the original Hebrew the word "radah" is used, which means, "to tread down".[2] This implies rulership in a more definitive way. It directs us to rule <u>over</u> the animals.

As we continue reading Genesis, we encounter the serpent, the craftiest of animals, who began speaking to Eve to try and deceive her. Genesis 3:5 says, "For God knows that when you eat of it your eyes will be opened, and you will be like God, knowing good and evil." The serpent is already trying to deceive her and give her a false sense of purpose by twisting the very words her Father spoke to her. Then the serpent also deceives Adam. Keep in mind Adam was given "dominion" over everything that moves in the earth. Yet he allowed him to not only be deceived by his wife but also by the serpent. He had already departed from the words and blessing given to himself and his wife because he failed to function in his creative purpose as outlined in Genesis 3:4-7. It was at this point that sin entered the world, not necessarily through the actual bite into the fruit but through the disobedience of not taking dominion over the serpent. Adam allowed the serpent to have authority over him! We know that the serpent is Satan and his very character is to rob, kill and destroy. He does, and he started with the first father of mankind. Our purpose for being created has never changed, but we have allowed ourselves to become so far removed from our purpose that we tend to blame the serpent instead of stepping into our God-given role of dominion. The only authority the enemy has is what <u>we</u> have given to him.

Jesus became the second Adam to restore all that the first Adam lost to sin. (Romans 5:12-21) Our purposes are reestablished because Christ came to show us the way and to reconcile us to the Father. Furthermore, our creative purpose has not changed. Jesus Himself showed us how to take dominion; now we must do our part and discover what role we are to play in this. To do this, we must first understand that we each have five spheres of influence: ourselves, our family, our church, our community, and our region. Yet how can we be influential in any spheres beyond ourselves if we are not yet able to rule over our own souls?

Proverbs 25:28 states, "He who *has* no rule over his own spirit *is like* a city broken down, without walls." (NKJV) We first need to take learn to take dominion over our own souls, to subject everything to the plans and purposes of the Father. The latter part of this book will lead you into the understanding of how to take dominion over your soul. This section will first show you what you were created to "BE".

### Read Genesis 1:26- 31; 2:7, 15-17; Genesis 3; Romans 5:12-21

1.    In whose image was man created? _____

2.    From what did the Lord form man, and how?

_____

_____

_____

3.    Where did the Lord put the man? _____

4.    What was he to do in the garden? _____

5.    How did the enemy twist God's words towards Eve? (Genesis 3:3-5) _____

6.  Romans 5:12 says that sin came into the world (finish the sentence)

    _____

    _____

7.  Therefore, as one trespass led to _____ for all men, so one act of _____ leads to justification and life for all men. (Romans 5:18)

8.  One trespass led to many being sinners but because of ONE led many _____.

### The Journey Outward into Being

As I started my healing journey, I discovered it was very difficult to learn to simply "Be" who I was called to be. I kept trying to be like others, to mimic them, not feeling comfortable in my own identity. Or I wanted to develop my identity through what I did. I was striving and never at peace. One day I realized I didn't have to strive to attain something that had already been given to me. It was as if I heard the Lord say, "Stop doing and start being". Once I could achieve "Being", I would find fruitfulness, multiplication, authority, and the power to take dominion. We need to fully rely on the scriptures that tell us what the Father who created us says we are. We do not have to follow God: we must become one with God, allowing his character and attributes to BE in us.

## Being fruitful and multiplying

Be fruitful and multiply; this is the first command given to Adam, as previously discussed. This means to bring forth, to increase, to grow… in abundance.

## Fill the earth

I challenge you with this one thought from the Lord's Prayer: "Your kingdom come, Your will be done, on earth as it is in heaven." (Matthew 6:10) Heaven is full of the glory of God and His presence permeates everything there. For His will to be done and His kingdom to come would be to fill the earth with His presence and manifest His glory. If we "fill" our first sphere of influence (ourselves) the filling can then spread to our other spheres of influence until the fullness of His presence reigns over all the earth.

## Subdue it

The word subdue comes from the Hebrew "kabash", which means "to conquer, to tread down, to bring into bondage by force."[2] This means that when the enemy tries to take what is yours, you must remember that the only authority he has is that which you yourself have given over to him.

*Father, help me to stop striving. Help me to learn to just "Be" in You and You in me. Show me how to begin to function out of that place of being to bring You glory in my spheres of influence.*

How does this apply to you? In what ways, do you need to BE in your own personal sphere? In the spheres of your family, church, community, and your region/state?

Begin to pray and ask the Lord about these areas of your life and journal what the Lord is saying to you.

_____

_____

_____

_____

_____

_____

_____

_____

_____

_____

_____

_____

_____

_____

_____

_____

_____

_____

_____

_____

_____

_____

_____

_____

_____

_____

_____

_____

_____

_____

_____

_____

_____

_____

**Bonding with the Father: His is our Creator**
- ❖     **Isaiah 40:28**
- ❖     **Isaiah 43:15**
- ❖     **Colossians 3:10**
- ❖     **1 Peter 4:19**

**Memorize:**

*"So, God created man in his own image, in the image of God he created him; male and female he created them" Genesis 1:27*

# Lesson 23 - Created to Be Fruitful and Multiply

*"...that you may walk worthy of the Lord, fully pleasing*
Him, *being fruitful in every good work and increasing in the*
*knowledge of God;"*
*Colossians 1:10 (NKJV)*

As we read in the previous chapter, one of the things God told Adam and Eve was to be fruitful and multiply. The Lord specifically implied that He purposed them to have children and grandchildren. Adam and Eve were not to be the only two people on earth. As we study the word "fruitful" throughout scriptures, its meaning changes in different contexts. Noah and his sons were told to repopulate the earth after the flood. Genesis 9:1 "So God blessed Noah and his sons, and said to them: 'Be fruitful and multiply, and fill the earth.'" (NKJV) Abram and his sons were told they would be fruitful and that nations would come from them. The blessing of fruitfulness encompassed more than population growth to include fruitfulness in the possession of land as well as wealth. When a Jewish father in the Bible passed on a blessing to his children it always included mention of fruitfulness and prosperity. In contrast, a woman who could not conceive a child was considered cursed with unfruitfulness.

In the New Testament, however, fruitfulness takes on a whole new meaning. Paul tells the Colossians to be fruitful in every good work. To the Galatians, Paul speaks of the fruit of the spirit. I say all this not to confuse the issue of fruitfulness but to show you that the Lord's intention for us is to be fruitful in every way and in every sphere that we are connected to, whether spiritual, physical, financial, or in childbearing. As Christians, we are also commanded to multiply that which the Lord has given to us. By speaking a blessing of fruitfulness and multiplication over our children, we are passing on the promises of the His covenant with us.

You are called to be fruitful and multiply in all five of your spheres of influence:

1.   **Yourself:** You are personally responsible to be fruitful within your own being. It is up to you to ask the Holy Spirit to help you be fruitful and multiply so you can grow spiritually. Galatians 5:22-24 states, "But the fruit of the Spirit is love, joy, peace, patience, kindness, goodness, faithfulness, gentleness, self-control; against such things there is no law. And those who belong to Christ Jesus have crucified the flesh with its passions and desires." Crucifying the flesh with its passions and desires is the primary fruit from which all other fruitfulness flows.

2.   **Your family**: It is up to us to help our families be fruitful in the Lord. This includes any family relationship within your sphere. It is your responsibility to be Jesus' hands and feet to them.

3.   **Your Church**: God wants our fruitfulness to multiply within the church as well. I want to emphasize here that we are _all_ called to spiritually reproduce. Jesus modeled what spiritual reproduction looks like. He commanded us to "Go therefore and make disciples of all nations, baptizing them in the name of the Father and of the Son and of the Holy Spirit, teaching them to observe all that I have commanded you. And

behold, I am with you always, to the end of the age."
(Matthew 28:19-20)

I want to challenge you with this thought: Jesus didn't say go into the world and make people come into your church to become converts; He told them to make disciples. A disciple is one who accepts and assists in the spreading of the doctrines of another. Jesus showed His disciples how to be like Him and then taught them how to reproduce His qualities in others. The word "Christian" thus implies "those who have Christ-like characteristics."[1] To take on certain characteristics, we need to be in relationship with someone who has them - Jesus Christ Himself. We have turned the word "Christian" into a religion when it really implies a relationship. As Christians we are to reproduce and make other Christians who are in a relationship with Jesus.

4.    **Your community**: This encompasses the places where you work, live, and do business (shop). We have incorrectly put "church" within "four walls" and confined it to a place where we "do" something, a building where we worship, teach, pray, serve. We are not supposed to confine our worship, teaching, prayers, and service among those we fellowship with once or twice a week but share them with everyone we meet in our daily lives, regardless of their race, gender, socioeconomic status, or occupation. At present, Sunday is the most segregated day of the week! This should not be so! We need to take our church with us into the world and bring the world into our church. It will be the Fruit of the Spirit evident in our lives that will draw others to want to be fruitful as well.

223

5.　**Region**: This is taking fruitfulness beyond our locality to our nation, and perhaps beyond, to the ends of the earth. I live in the city of Cleveland; my community is a small section of the city, but my region is North East Ohio. The Lord has begun connecting us with people of like minds and kingdom visions for making not just our city fruitful but our corner of Ohio fruitful as well. When you feel called to impact your region, pray and ask the Lord for the boundaries of your region.

These five spheres represent ministry on earth. When we become filled with the fullness of Christ, we become conduits of His fruitfulness. This is appealing and contagious and spreads like the church in the book of Acts, which "increased in numbers daily". (Acts 16:5)

**Read John 15**

1.　What does Jesus say happens to the one who does not bear fruit?

　　_____

2.　Jesus shows us that the only way to bear fruit is to?

　　_____

3.　In v. 5 Jesus says, "Whoever abides in Me and I in him, he it is that bears _____fruit, for apart from _____ you can do _____."

4.　Jesus gives us a promise of abiding in v. 7. What is that promise? _____

5. Jesus says, we are His _____ if we do whatever He commands us. v. 14

6. In v. 16, what did Jesus say He choose us to do?

_____

### The Journey Outward: Sharing the Journey with Others

As we just read, it is not enough for us to become who we are supposed to be and then rest; we are to share the journey with others. Beginning to impart to others what you have received in your healing is part of the process of walking into wholeness. This sharing is an ongoing process of growing and then sharing and then growing some more. You can only share and impart that which you have experienced yourself. Being hidden away with the Lord, or as we just studied in John 15, abiding in Jesus, is a safe place, and you may not want to leave. But much like a baby cannot stay in the womb and continue to grow, neither can you be in a hidden place and continue to grow in your fruitfulness. You must begin your outward journey and teach others what you have learned. You may begin with members of your family. You may begin sharing with someone at church or with a neighbor. People may even notice a transformation in you and ask why you look or seem different. People used to ask me if I had lost weight; I had, but it was spiritual weight, not physical weight. Their questions, however, allowed me to begin sharing what God was doing in me, and that birthed in me the desire to help others in their healing journeys. If you don't allow yourself to become fearful, but remain obedient to the Lord's purposes, this will become a natural progression of outward growth and fruitfulness.

**Answer these questions as you journal:**

Are you fulfilling His purposes? Are you seeing fruit in your ministry? If not, why? What must you do to be more fruitful? What does the Lord want you to do to be more fruitful in ministry?

_____

_____

_____

_____

_____

_____

_____

_____

_____

_____

_____

_____

_____

_____

_____

_____

_____

_____

_____

_____

_____

_____

_____

_____

_____

_____

_____

_____

Let's pray:

*Father, I worship you through the blood of your Son, Jesus. I desire to be fruitful in every sphere of my life. I want to see Your kingdom be fruitful so that You will be glorified through me. You have put me here for a purpose; show me, Lord, what my role is and how you have created me to be fruitful in this realm.*

**Bonding with the Father: Promises of Fruitfulness**
❖ **Jeremiah 23:3**
❖ **Isaiah 32:16**
❖ **Genesis 28:3**
❖ **Leviticus 26:9**
❖ **Psalm 107:37-38**

**Memorize:**

*"Until the Spirit is poured upon us from on high, and the wilderness becomes a fruitful field, and the fruitful field is valued as a forest." Isaiah 32:15 (AMPC)*

# Lesson 24 - Created to Possess the Land

*"Pass through the midst of the camp and command the people, 'Prepare your provisions, for within three days you are to pass over this Jordan to go in to take possession of the land that the LORD your God is giving you to possess.'"*
*Joshua 1:11*

In Genesis, as you read the promises that the Lord made to Abraham (Genesis 12-22) you discover that God told Abraham to leave his home. God did not tell Abraham where he was going but lead him step by step. Because of Abraham's obedience, God said He would bless him and his descendants that his descendants would be as numerous as the sands on the seashore and the stars in the heavens. Due to a severe famine, Abraham's early descendants (Jacob, his twelve sons, and their families) settled in Egypt and populated that land. Pharaoh, King of Egypt, saw how these people were growing in number, and out of fear of an uprising he held them as slaves in great oppression. The Lord never intended for His people to stay in Egypt; He had made a promise to them – a land covenant – that they would inherit and inhabit a specific geographical area. So, the Lord raised up Moses to take the Israelites out of Egypt (Exodus 2-14) and into the Promised Land. But after their escape, the Israelites continually complained and lived in constant fear and mistrust. The years of living as oppressed slaves under a harsh king had caused them to mistrust the promises of the Lord, even amidst the fulfillment of those promises; abuse and mistreatment produces distrust, which can lead to mistrust in the future.

(Exodus 6:8-9 or Numbers 14:11) God revealed His power to fulfill His promises through multiple miracles and He revealed His grace and mercy with every "second chance" He gave them, yet the Israelites continued to pull away from Him.

Finally, while in the wilderness as they neared their promised land, the Israelites rebelled yet again. Because of their rebellion, (Numbers 14:20-22) mistrust, and fear, they had tested God one too many times. This time the Lord told His people that they were going to wander in the wilderness another 40 years, until that rebellious generation had passed away. (Numbers 32:13) He knew that if He gave this ungrateful generation the land, they would not be satisfied nor would they bring honor or glory to Him for giving them the land.

**The Next Generation**

After 40 years, a new generation was birthed that had not experienced the fear of men but knew the fear of God. This generation had only lived in peace and provision. They did not have the scars of slavery on their backs; they only knew the stories of the past. A new leader arose as Moses passed his mantle of leadership to Joshua. Joshua was from the older generation, one of the few who had remained faithful to follow God's instructions through Moses. After Moses died, the new generation was ready to step in and take dominion of the Promised Land. (The book of Joshua gives an account of this generation.)

As during the time of Moses' leadership, the Israelites crossed through a parted body of water that signified their salvation and baptism. The first action performed after crossing the Jordan into the Promised Land was circumcising all the men. Until then, this generation had not known circumcision. This purification rite was performed in preparation to take dominion of the land and its inhabitants, opponents of God who had defiled the land. God wanted the land to be purified.

When God created mankind, He ordained in man that they were to possess land. But then sin entered the world and the land itself became defiled. The land had to be retaken and subdued, brought into submission by force. Once you have taken over and have control, then you are to take dominion over the land, which means to rule and maintain control. I believe we are being asked to establish God's Kingdom here, by spiritual warfare, to fight to maintain what God has given us.

As His children, we are called to govern the land the King has given to us. Again, going back into our spheres of influence, we are called to keep in step with Holy Spirit so that we can be fruitful in our families and other areas. Like our brothers and sisters before us, we have allowed the enemy to come into our spheres of influence so that, little by little, we have begun to lose our authority and dominion. Just like Adam, we have allowed the serpent to come in and feed us lies that cause us to hand over the ground that God has given us. We need to understand that like in Exodus, God gives his people multiple chances to step into their place of authority spiritually, or they will lose their rights to inherit the land. We need to learn from them and not just judge them.

**Read Judges 1-2:6**

1. What was the first thing the people did before they went into battle? (Judges 1:3) _____

2. The tribes learned to fight together; what two tribes fought together? _____

3. What did Caleb offer to the one who captured Kiriath-sepher?

_____

4. Caleb's daughter recognized she had an inheritance coming and she was not afraid to ask for it. For what did she ask?

_____

_____

5. In Judges 1:19, what lands did they capture?

_____

6. Judges 1:20-36 there was only one person who drove out the people who inhabited the land. Who was it?

_____

_____

7.   In Chapter 2:1-6, what was the consequence of not totally evicting the enemies from the land?

_____

_____

### *The Journey Outward: Created to Possess*

The Israelites were accustomed to taking land from their enemies and regaining control. However, they did not complete the task; they did not remove or destroy everyone as the Lord had commanded. Consequently, they had to continue battling to keep and maintain their land and to prevent themselves from being influenced and corrupted by those they had allowed to remain. Because of this, the remnants became thorns in the Israelite's sides and their gods became a snare for Israel.

It is shocking how subtle the enemy can be. Have you noticed that over the years television shows have increasingly shown sex and violence? I am amazed at what we call comedy these days and what we have accepted. (I am using television as one example among many.) Christians sit by and allow it while our culture becomes increasingly morally depraved. The very character of the serpent breathes subtlety.

Christians are responsible to guard the places the Lord has given to us, to both subdue and maintain them for Him. If you read the book of Judges, you will see the cycle of losing and gaining ground, all because of the things the Israelites had allowed to subtly come in their lives. Gained ground that is not maintained begins to influence and take control of the people, instead of the other way around, and they come under the bondage all over again.

The Lord wants to trust you with the things He wants to give to you. He wants you to subdue and take dominion. You are created to possess areas of influence, including land. This includes a company you may own, or your job, or the house you own or rent. He has given you a place to manage and take responsibility for. Have you allowed yourself to be deceived into thinking you have no authority in these areas?

Let's Pray

*Heavenly Father, through Your blood I worship You and ask that You apply the atoning Blood of Jesus to the roots of all my spheres of influence. Show me areas where I have not properly handled that which You have given me. I repent that I have allowed the Serpent to deceive me and that I have given away my authority in _____ (name areas) to the enemy that Jesus has won back for me. Father, forgive me for giving in to this lie and deception. Forgive me for seeing myself as a victim of the enemy instead of the victor You have made me to be in Christ. Father, show me where You desire me to walk in the fullness of the authority You have given me. Thank you that Jesus has won this back from the enemy for me.*

Now take time, again, to examine all the spheres of influence we discussed in the previous chapters where you have allowed the enemy to have dominion instead of you taking authority. Journal what you hear the Lord say and then repent of anything He shows you.

Ask the Lord to show you the strategy for regaining that area back for His glory.

_____

_____

_____

_____

_____

_____

_____

_____

_____

_____

_____

_____

_____

_____

_____

_____

_____

_____

_____

_____

_____

_____

_____

_____

_____

_____

_____

_____

_____

_____

_____

**Bonding with the Father: He Rules**
- ❖ **Exodus 15:18**
- ❖ **Psalm 47:8**
- ❖ **Psalm 93:1**
- ❖ **Psalm 146:10**
- ❖ **Luke 1:33**
- ❖ **Revelation 19:6**

**Memorize:**

*"that He worked in Christ when He raised Him from the dead and seated Him at His right hand in the heavenly places, far above all rule and authority and power and dominion, and above every name that is named, not only in this age but also in the one to come. And He put all things under his feet and gave him as head over all things to the church," Ephesians 1:20-22*

# Chapter 9

# Manifesting His Glory

# Lesson 25 - Called to Represent

*" Nor will people say, Look! Here [it is]! or, See, [it is] there! For behold,* **the kingdom of God is within you [in your hearts] and among you [surrounding you].***"*
*Luke 17:21(AMPC) [emphasis added]*

Have you ever heard the song "Father's Eyes" by Amy Grant? I used to love singing that song, and it became like a prayer to me. I had always been told I looked like my earthly dad. But when I came to know the Lord, what I really desired was to look like my Heavenly Father; I wanted everything about me to reflect God. I have plain brown eyes, not the type that would receive compliments, and wondered if anyone would ever see Jesus in my eyes.

In June 2006, my family and 18 other people from Cleveland (OH) went to Guatemala on a mission trip. The first weekend we attended a conference, and the following Monday, we had an opportunity to pray with the national staff from Campus Crusade for Christ (now known as CRU). The group was surprised when we showed up because they are used to sending missions teams out to do ministry, not bringing missions teams in to pray for them! We spent two wonderful days interceding and getting to know this staff. At the end of our time there, the head of the organization stood up to share his heartfelt appreciation towards us. He shared how deeply he was touched and ministered to. He said that some of us touched him with our words and some of us touched him with our intercession.

He also said that he was ministered to just by looking into our eyes and seeing the love of Jesus. When he said that he was looking directly at me! I thought nothing of it until we all got in line to shake hands with him personally. As I approached him, in his broken English he said to me, "I see much in your eyes." I said, "I hope it is good?" and he replied with tears, "I see Jesus in your eyes..." Now I was crying! In that moment, I was reminded of the song that I had often prayed for myself and thanked God for His goodness to me.

How exciting it is to know that when we receive Christ as Savior, the kingdom of God is already within us. Yet many of us still walk around as if we are all alone and doing things on our own. We forget that we are called to represent the living God every moment of our lives.

1 Corinthians 10:31 states, "So, whether you eat or drink, or whatever you do, do all to the glory of God." Jesus never forgot what He was sent here to do. Even as a young boy He was doing His Father's work. At the age of twelve, He stayed behind in Jerusalem to talk with the rabbis following his family's annual Passover pilgrimage. His parents did not realize that He had not left with the caravan, and when they went back, they found Him sitting in the temple complex talking intelligently with the teachers. (Luke 2:41-46) When His parents confronted Him, He said to them, "How is it that you had to look for Me? Did you not see *and* know that it is necessary [as a duty] for Me to be in My Father's house *and* [occupied] about My Father's business? (Luke 2:49-50) (AMPC).

Jesus knew He came to represent His Father and attend to His business. We, too, are to be about our Father's business. We need to understand the magnitude of the call and responsibility we have on our lives. We must understand that we have a job to do and that it should be our first priority. Matthew 5:16 commands us to "Let your light so shine before men, that they may see your good works and glorify your Father in Heaven." (NKJV)

To manifest the glory of the Father, we need to first recognize that it is a command. We need to know that the kingdom of God is within us and that everything we do must reflect the attributes of the One who sent us. We should be like a conduit, so that His glory can flow into us and then out of us to others. Remember, the purpose of taking dominion is not just to take control, but also to bring transformation to a community so that it will begin to reflect the glory of the Lord.

The more you allow the Lord to transform you from the inside out, the more His glory can radiate through you. You are a "God carrier, Jesus incarnate"! The Glory of the Living God is manifested in your being so that every part of the community that you represent reflects the magnificent beauty of the Living God. Whatever you touch or encounter is affected because the Glory of the Lord is in you. I really hope you get a clear picture of this truth. I think sometimes we go through life numb to the world, not realizing that our touch, our smile, our eyes, and the way we act towards others all make a difference to the Lord. Everything we do should be determined by whether it brings honor to the Lord.

2 Corinthians 2:14-15 states, "But thanks be to God, who in Christ always leads us in triumphal procession, and **through**

us **spreads the fragrance of the knowledge of him everywhere**. For **we are the aroma of Christ** to God among those who are being saved and among those who are perishing." [emphasis added] How awesome is that! We are the aroma, the sweet-smelling fragrance of Christ to others! Jesus says in John 17:4 "I have brought glory to You here on earth by doing everything You gave me to do." (CEV) How do we bring our Heavenly Father glory? By doing everything He gives us to do.

**Read John 17**

1.   Whom did Jesus seek to glorify? _____

2.   How did Jesus bring the Father glory? (v. 4-5)

_____

_____

3.   Who was Jesus praying for in v. 9?

_____

4.   In v. 11, what does Jesus pray we would be?

_____

5.   In v. 13 Jesus prays that…

_____

6.   Jesus does not pray that the Father would take us out of the world but that He would keep us from what?

_____

7.   What is it that Jesus asks the Father for on our behalf?

v. 22 _____

### The Journey Outward: Being a Conduit of His Glory

In what ways do you need to be more consciously aware of your surroundings and of whom you are representing? What actions do you need to take? These are just a few of the questions we should be asking the Lord about ourselves.

Imagine that you have undergone the glorification process just as Jesus did at the Mount of Transfiguration. His whole countenance was transformed. When people looked at Him they were drawn to Him. This was not a movie star persona; Jesus didn't do things to please himself. He only did what He saw the Father doing. Just as Jesus found his identity in the Father, we are to find our identity in Christ. Please look at the "In Christ" list found in the back of this book and begin to declare one each day. You can even post them on note cards around your house.

Let's pray:

*Heavenly Father,*

*I now see that I am to reflect You. Just as the moon reflects the sun in nature, just as Jesus reflects the nature of the Father, I am to reflect You. I desire to reflect You but I must confess I have not been a good representative. Father, please reveal all the ways I have reflected the opposite of who You are.*

Write down in your journal any ways in which you have negatively reflected Christ by your words or actions and have been a poor representative of Him.

Spend time in prayer and repentance.

_____

_____

_____

_____

_____

_____

_____

_____

_____

_____

_____

_____

_____

_____

_____

_____

_____

_____

_____

_____

_____

_____

_____

_____

_____

_____

_____

_____

_____

_____

_____

_____

_____

_____

_____

**Bonding with the Father: He is Glorious**
- ❖     **Exodus 15:6**
- ❖     **Psalm 76:4**
- ❖     **Psalm 145:5, 12**
- ❖     **Isaiah 4:2**

**Memorize:**

_"The Lord and the Spirit are one and the same, and the Lord's Spirit sets us free. So our faces are not covered. They show the bright glory of the Lord, as the Lord's Spirit makes us more like our glorious Lord." 2 Corinthians 3:17-18 (CEV)_

# Lesson 26 - Root out, Pull down, Build and Plant

*"See, I have this day appointed you to the oversight of the nations and of the kingdoms to root out and pull down, to destroy and to overthrow, to build and to plant."*
*Jeremiah 1:10 (AMPC)*

When the Lord first led me to study this verse years ago, I began asking Him many questions. I have learned that part of our authority to subdue and take dominion involves the very process Jeremiah talks about in this verse. A lot is required in all the spheres of our authority as discussed in the last chapter.

It is important to remember that we cannot uproot sin out of the last sphere (your community) until we uproot sin in the first sphere (ourselves). Pulling the roots out of our souls makes way for the glory of the Lord to be manifested in us. Colossians 1:27 says, "To them God willed to make known what are the riches of the glory of this mystery among the Gentiles: which is Christ in you, the hope of glory." (NKJV) It is Christ in us that is the hope of the manifested glory in the earth. But it cannot start in our region until it starts in us.

One of the sins that prevents the full manifestation of His glory is pride. Webster defines "pride" as "inordinate self-esteem; an unreasonable conceit of one's own superiority in talents, beauty, wealth, accomplishments, rank, or elevation in office, which manifests itself in lofty airs, distance, reserve, and often in contempt of others".[1] It was Satan's pride that caused him to fall. (Isaiah 14:13-15) It is pride that keeps us relationally separated from others relationally. If we were to truly pay attention to our language we would begin to hear how many times we say "I, me, my". God desires His children to walk in unity in every aspect of our lives. The root of pride runs so deep and is woven in so much of our lives that often we are not even aware of it. If asked, many of us would believe that we are not walking in it because it has remained a hidden sin issue. The enemy will use this tactic to make us think that we are innocent of this sin. If we were to walk out of pride and into true unity, we would be walking in a greater revelation of Christ in us, the Hope of Glory. God is waiting for us to reveal who we are to creation so that the whole earth would be filled with His glory. As we root out pride within our selves and our relationships, it will no longer be "I" who is living but Christ in us! How exciting is that!

### Rooting out Pride in our Relationships

My husband Mike and I thought we understood the scripture, "Can two walk together unless they are agreed?" (Amos 3:3) (NKJV) One day the Lord said to me, "April, pay attention to how you and Mike physically walk together." I was amazed to notice that when we walk, I tend to at a walk faster pace than he does. The Lord said, "This is how the two of you walk out life. You need to learn to walk together in agreement, because where there is agreement, I am there." (Matthew 18:19) The Lord showed us that it was our pride that kept us from walking in agreement with each other and with God himself. God revealed to us that we felt that what one of us heard from the Lord was more important that what the other one heard from the Lord. We had to ask the Lord where the pride was in each of us individually as well as within our marriage. He then showed us how we had compartmentalized our lives: his company, my job, his ministry, my ministry. By the time we realized this, we had been married 22 years and now had 22 years' worth of pride manifesting as individualism, which could have led to separation. As we allowed God to root out pride, we began to love each other deeper because we were no longer rejecting each other.

Since that day, the Lord has changed the way we do ministry and how we relationally handle many aspects. Now we choose to spend time in prayer and not move forward in a decision until we agree. I have slowed my pace, and Mike is walking faster. It's been a beautiful picture of the body of Christ as the bride of Christ, coming into right alignment as we submit ourselves to Him and each other.

**Read Romans 8:1-30**

1.   According to v. 5-6, what should we set our mind on?

_____

2.   If we walk in the flesh can we still please God? _____

3.   You do not walk in the flesh if _____ dwells in you.

4.   If you live by the flesh what will happen to you? v. 13

_____

_____

5.   Those who are led by the Spirit are

_____

_____

6.    According to v. 18-23 what is longing for the sons of God to manifest? _____

### *The Journey Outward: Manifesting His Glory*

Pride keeps us self-focused and not God-focused. It causes us to reject others and keeps us in a place of isolation and independence. All creation is longing for the sons of God to manifest His glory; what are you manifesting? Are you walking in fleshly desires or are you walking in the Spirit? Unless pride is rooted out and torn down, we cannot begin to build and plant. It is when we finally die to self and root out pride that we will no longer see jealousy in the body of Christ, but true unity. James 3:16 says, "For where envy and self-seeking *exist*, confusion and every evil thing *are* there." (NKJV) Self-seeking, jealousy, and envy are all rooted in pride, and according to this verse in James, it invites confusion and invites the presence of the enemy.

Let's pray and ask the Holy Spirit to root out our pride!

*Father, I worship You through the blood of Jesus, and because of who You are in us, I ask that You show me the ways I am living in pride through my flesh. Please forgive me for walking in my flesh by being attention seeking, being jealous (continue repenting of the pride He shows you) _____. I give you full permission to pull out every root of pride, to tear down the old mind-sets that come along with them so that You can begin to build relationships and plant unity. I pray that as You root this out, that You begin to release a greater measure of Jesus Christ within me so that I can "BE" the Hope of Glory that all creation is longing for.*

Now begin to journal any areas of pride that Holy Spirit reveals to you, and continue to pray and root it out as we prayed above. If the Lord leads you, repent of the pride in your family, congregations, neighborhoods, region, and nation.

_____

_____

_____

_____

_____

_____

_____

_____

_____

_____

_____

_____

_____

_____

_____

_____

_____

_____

_____

_____

_____

_____

_____

_____

_____

_____

_____

_____

**Bonding with the Father: Master Builder**
- ❖ **Psalm 69:35**
- ❖ **Psalm 127:1**
- ❖ **Jeremiah 24:6**
- ❖ **Jeremiah 31:4**
- ❖ **1 Corinthians 3:10**

**Memorize:**

*I have been crucified with Christ. It is no longer I who live, but Christ who lives in me. And the life I now live in the flesh I live by faith in the Son of God, who loved me and gave himself for me. Galatians 2:20*

# Lesson 27 - Places of Humility

*Whoever exalts himself [with haughtiness and empty pride] shall be humbled (brought low), and whoever humbles himself [whoever has a modest opinion of himself and behaves accordingly] shall be raised to honor.*
*Matthew 23:12* (AMPC)

Pride in our hearts is ongoing and is an area we need to continually allow the Lord to keep in check. God hates pride so much that He says in Proverbs 16:18, "Pride goes before destruction, and a haughty spirit before a fall." What we don't realize is how pride is masked differently in each of us. In this lesson, I hope to share with you two different and subtle forms of pride under the disguise of false humility.

In 2007, I recall receiving many emails from various people calling the Body of Christ in America to a time of fasting and prayer, as the Lord was calling this nation to a time of prayer and humbling. 2 Chronicles 7:14 says, "if My people who are called by My name <u>humble themselves and pray and seek My face and turn from their wicked ways,</u> then I will hear from heaven and will forgive their sin and heal their land." [emphasis added] Mike and I knew this was something in which we had to participate. Prior to the fast, I believe I heard the Lord say, "I am taking My Body through a season of humility, lest they be humiliated." It was during this season that I injured my back while on vacation. I heard the Lord say that He would heal it when the time of fasting was over. No matter what I did, whether sitting or standing, the most comfortable position was face down on all four limbs. My husband would chuckle as he walked into a room, seeing me on all fours trying to bring relief to my back. During this

253

season, I found such a sweet place with the Lord as I worshiped Him in this position! He was breaking off pride and presumption and giving me abundant grace to teach me true humility.

Have you ever heard the saying, "The bigger they are the harder they fall?" Unfortunately, there were well-known Christian pastors whose sins were exposed during this same season. God was showing us that a humble character must accompany a great calling. If you do not allow God to humble you and deal with your character, He cannot trust you with the calling He has for you. The Lord began showing Mike and I that we needed to be in a place of humility, and that became our desire. We cried out, "Lord, humble us. Keep us low, so that You will be exalted."

It was during this season that the Lord gave Mike a message called "Humility and Humiliation" The root word in both is "humble". *Webster's Dictionary* defines "humble" as "not haughty or proud; not arrogant or assertive; reflecting, expressing, or offered in a spirit of deference or submission."[1]

The Word is clear that His righteous judgment will come to the House of God first. (1 Peter 4:17) Our Heavenly Father has given us a standard of Holiness. He will not compromise. Holiness is humility; anything other than that is exalting ourselves above Jesus… "And being found in human form, he humbled himself by becoming obedient to the point of death, even death on a cross." (Philippians 2:8)

There cannot be room for pride. As I mentioned earlier God hates pride. Greater intimacy and power are cultivated in humility. If God chooses to move you into notoriety, the battle will be to maintain that place of humility. If you make choices that are not godly, and if you have not submitted to the warnings of encroaching pride, it is guaranteed that God will put you in your place through humiliation. We are not above consequences or repercussions; just because we have God's forgiveness doesn't mean we have access to it when we are blatantly exalting ourselves.

If God is not getting the glory for what we do in the private times, He is not getting the glory for the work being done in the open either. He will be sure to expose sin we commit in private. Ephesians 5:11-14 states, "Take no part in the unfruitful works of darkness, but instead expose them. For it is shameful even to speak of the things that they do in secret. But when anything is exposed by the light, it becomes visible, for anything that becomes visible is light."

Let's look at the story of the prophet Nathan being sent by God to speak to King David. (2 Samuel 12) It was in the pride of being the King, and his resulting ability to get anything he wanted, that David helped himself to another man's wife. It was his pride that kept him from wanting to go out and fight in the first place, in complete defiance of what Kings were supposed to do. Instead of serving his people by leading the troops into battle, he became self-serving and prideful.

David did repent, but he still lost the son Bathsheba bore to him. Because David repented, God restored and gave him another son, Solomon, who became a great king that ruled the kingdom for a long time. Had David not chosen to submit to God, we can hardly imagine the repercussions that might have occurred.

One of the ways pride disguises itself is in false humility. There are two types of false humility; both examples are masked in insecurity and low self-esteem. There is the false humility with which most of us are familiar: when given a compliment, the recipient fishes for more. For example, "The message you taught was so powerful." "Well thank you, I just threw that together at the last minute." "Oh! You seemed so prepared I thought you had worked on that for weeks! You are so talented!"

The other disguise is giving the impression of humility by using religious activities. This occurs when a person is preoccupied with their failings and is more an outward appearance of religiousness, but the words and actions do not line up with the true heart. I love this quote from C.S. Lewis: "Humility is not thinking less of yourself; it is thinking of yourself less." [2]

The Bible gives an example of this in the parable of the tax collector who is truly humbling himself before God versus the Pharisee who thinks he is humbling himself before God but is only going through the religious motions. (Luke 18:10-14) One of the characteristics of false humility is that it tears others down by exalting oneself, where true humility builds others up. I love the saying, "[a] humble leader looks in the mirror, not out the window." Our unwillingness to humble ourselves privately amidst His discipline towards us can result in giving God no choice but to bring discipline through humiliation.

It's the desire of God's heart for us to walk in humility because then He receives the glory when He does something through us, not us. To truly manifest His glory, we need to choose to humble ourselves as Jesus did.

Jesus warned his disciples about pride. Often, when we begin to experience the manifest power of God moving through us as the disciples did, it is easy for us to fall prey to prideful thoughts. We begin to think that we had more to do with what happened than God did. God can use whomsoever He wants, whenever He wants; He will use the one who is walking in the greatest humility before He uses someone who is walking in pride.

## Read Matthew 20:20-28 & Galatians 5:19-24

1.    Who was it that approached Jesus to ask for her sons to sit at His right and left hand in the kingdom? _____

2.    Who did He say was the only one who could make that decision to sit with Him (v. 23)? _____

3.    What happened when the other disciples heard about her request?

_____

_____

4.    What did Jesus say should be done to be great?

_____

5.    In Galatians 5:21, what does Paul say will not happen if they continue to walk in the flesh?

_____

_____

6.    List the fruits of the Spirit:

_____

_____

_____

7.    What are those who belong to Christ suppose to do with their lust and passions? _____

## *The Journey Outward: Manifesting His Glory in humility*

Although the Lord will give multiple warnings, we do not know how many He will give before He decides to discipline us. If we do not choose to humble ourselves, He will allow us to be humiliated. I would rather choose to submit and confess my sin to a person whom I can trust than to be humiliated. How about you? Journal your thoughts and ask the Lord for the gift of humility. Then spend time in worship.

_____

_____

_____

_____

_____

_____

_____

_____

_____

_____

_____

_____

_____

_____

_____

_____

_____

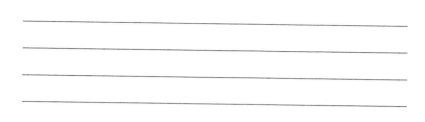

Let's pray:

*Father, I want to be like the tax collector and have a true heart of humility. I need you to show me every area of both false humility and pride. I give you permission to reveal all root issues of these sins You hate. You have called us to BE holy because You are holy. I choose Your holiness and righteousness. Thank You Lord for the places of humility that You bring me into; I know it is for my own good and protection. I choose to remain in this place and grow in humility until You desire to exalt me in Your timing.*

**Bonding with the Father: He is Humble**
- **Job 36:5**
- **Job 37:23**
- **Psalm 45:4**
- **1 Peter 5:5**
- **Isaiah 57:15**

**Memorize:**

*"For by the grace given to me I say to everyone among you not to think of himself more highly than he ought to think, but to think with sober judgment, each according to the measure of faith that God has assigned." Romans 12:3*

# Chapter 10

# Manifesting His Presence

# Lesson 28 - Walking in Unity

*"And day after day **they regularly assembled in the temple with united purpose**, and in their homes, they broke bread [including the Lord's Supper]. They partook of their food with gladness and simplicity and generous hearts,"*
Acts 2:46 (AMPC) [emphasis added]

In the excitement of discovering who we are, we often forget that it's not just about <u>what</u> we are called to do but also <u>with whom</u> we are called to do it. It's amazing that the people we are called to walk with in ministry are the very ones the enemy will use to bring division. Whether it is through hurt feelings or feelings of rejection (ours or theirs), we need to fight for that which God has entrusted to us. This division, caused by the enemy, is why so many in the Body of Christ, who were called to work together, separate from each other and tend to become isolated.

The scriptures are full of God telling us to be unified and walk as one. We preach it, but we don't want to live it for fear of being hurt. If we were rejected when we were young, our rejection will carry over into other relationships and cause us to isolate. The enemy will throw things at us: some of it is our stuff, some is the other person's stuff and other things are just the enemy's torment. The hard part is discerning which is which and sorting it all out. The closer we walk in what God has created us to walk in, the more it seems that irritants get in the way. Walking in unity is about walking in a level of maturity that causes us to deal with our wounds, and to love and forgive others despite their wounds.

263

This lesson was birthed from these experiences. We are called to "devote ourselves to the apostles' teaching and fellowship, to the breaking of bread and to prayer" just as the disciples did in Acts chapter 2. The outworking of this is found in verse 44 where "all who believed were together and had all things in common." If you look at this verse, what happened when they "devoted" themselves to these things? "Awe came upon every soul, and many wonders and signs were being done through them." (v. 43) *Webster's Dictionary* defines "devoted" as "to remain constant or committed through a solemn act."[1]

I see this like a marriage covenant, not just with the Lord but also with those with whom we are called to serve. Too many churches split for one reason or another. The divorce rate is worse inside the church than it is outside the church.[3] Part of humbling ourselves, as we shared in the last lesson, is about giving up our right to be correct all the time and to esteem other people better ourselves.

Acts 2:44 states, "they had all things in common." They shared everything with each other. If I had it and you needed it, it was given to you, and vice versa. As we continue to study this further, we will see that the disciples were happy, generous people who lived life praising God, and He added to their numbers daily! They had no needs; God supplied it all.

To "have all things in common" meant that their possessions were not their own but gifts from God to be shared as needed. This included not just material possessions but spiritual gifts as well. Our spiritual gifts are not "ours" but are gifts from God to be shared with others. If we are not sharing our gifts with others, using them for their good, we are being selfish.

Our gifts are not to build us up, but "...for building up the body of Christ, until we all attain to the unity of the faith and of the knowledge of the Son of God, to mature manhood, to the measure of the stature of the fullness of Christ..." (Ephesians 4:12b -13)

Our spiritual gifts are to be used for those we minister to as well. "There are different ways to serve the same Lord, and we can each do different things. Yet the same God works in all of us and helps us in everything we do. The Spirit has given each of us a special way of serving others." (1 Corinthians 12:5-7 CEV) [emphasis added] We have been holding onto our gifts and not using them for others and alongside others. Is it any wonder we are not walking together as we should in the same power and authority as the disciples?

It is God's heart to have the Body of Christ, the sons of God, living in true humility and esteeming one another in unity, serving one another with their gifts from God. This is part of the restoration process that all creation has been groaning for since The Fall.

### Read 1 Corinthians 12:14-26 & Philippians 2:3-5

1.    Who arranges the members of the body together as He chooses? _____

2.    Is there any part of the body that you do not need?

_____

3.    If one part of your body suffers do other suffer?

_____

4.  Is there to be any division in the body? _____

5.  Philippians 2:3 says we are not to do anything out of

    _____ or _____

6.  Whose interests are we to be looking out for?

    _____

7.  What should our attitude be like?

    _____

### *The Journey Outward: Walking in Unity*

If you are not doing and being who you are supposed to be in Christ, I cannot do and be who I am supposed to be. I cannot be a hand if you are not an arm to help connect me to the body; and what good am I being a hand without fingers, too?

I have had four surgeries on my left knee. When my knee acts up and doesn't do what it is supposed to do, my hip and back begin to feel pain. If my hip and back feel pain, I might as well sit down or go to bed because I can't do anything around the house. My husband Mike told me about Jack Lambert, who played linebacker for the Pittsburg Steelers in the 1980's. During one game, he injured his big toe and was out the rest of the season. When asked if he would come back to play next year, without hesitation he said, "Yes". The next year he started practicing and discovered that he could not get down on the line like he used to. He ended up quitting football that season all because of his big toe.[3] It sounds silly, but he was of no use to the team because of it.

Romans 8:19 "For [even the whole] creation (all nature) waits expectantly *and* longs earnestly for God's sons to be made known [waits for the revealing, the disclosing of their sonship]. (AMPC) I am part of creation and I am eagerly expecting you, as sons of God, to recognize your sonship in God. Once you do that, rejection will fall away and you will recognize your gifts, your authority, and move in His power!

*Father, please show me where I am not walking in unity my relationships. Show me my part in the sin of division, selfishness, anger, jealousy or greed that I have allowed in these relationships. Forgive me for giving up on a relationship because of hurts or frustrations and keeping the gifts you gave me to myself because of the hurts I experienced. Forgive me for my feelings of rejection from others and any lies I believed associated with them. I forgive _____ for their rejection towards me whether real or perceived.*

Journal what you are hearing and spend time in worship.

_____

_____

_____

_____

_____

_____

_____

_____

_____

_____

_____

_____

_____

_____

_____

_____

_____

_____

_____

_____

_____

**Bonding with the Father: God is One**
- ❖ **Isaiah 45:18**
- ❖ **Mark 12:29, 32-33**
- ❖ **John 17:20-21**
- ❖ **James 2:19**

**Memorize:**

*May the God of endurance and encouragement grant you to live in such harmony with one another, in accord with Christ Jesus, that together you may with one voice glorify the God and Father of our Lord Jesus Christ. Romans 15:5-6*

# Lesson 29 - Knowing your Gifts

*"Now there are varieties of gifts, but the same Spirit; and there are varieties of service, but the same Lord; and there are varieties of activities, but it is the same God who empowers them all in everyone."*
*1 Corinthians 12:4-6*

In my many years of being a Christian, one of the areas I was most excited to learn about was discovering my spiritual gifts and how to use them. It wasn't until I started coming under the proper spiritual head covering that I began to know what my gifts were and to receive the proper training to use them. In the past I had taken many spiritual gifting tests, but I found that they were based more on emotions and could change as one matured. There isn't anything wrong with these kinds of tests. They are a helpful tool; I just felt that they never really helped me. It took someone who had a good understanding of spiritual gifts to help me walk in mine with confidence and not be jealous of the ones I didn't have. Instead I learned how to appreciate the ones I did have.

As a very young Christian, I remember talking with a mature woman about things I would see and "know" about people. I was very in tune with certain spiritual beings, both angelic and demonic, and it would scare me because others around me we not seeing what I was seeing. Through this person, I discovered I had the gift of discernment of spirits; I just thought I was seeing things! Some years later, when I was part of an intercessory prayer team at our church, we did a prayer walk around the church, and I began to see the different spiritual gifts in operation. One would have had dreams, one would confirm through a word of knowledge, to another a word of prophecy had been given about the same situation. As we did this prayer assignment, I would get unexplainable odors or I would hear the Lord say, "this is the spirit of..." and He would name the spirit. I would see an object and discern how it was used in false worship. I have been in the midst of prayer and seen angels and demons at war and have begun praying for the battle. If I walked by a person, the Lord would tell me what kind of demons were tormenting them and show me how to pray. I could walk somewhere and begin to feel a headache or nausea or tightness in my chest; I would ask the Lord "what is this?" and He would tell me what kind of defilement was in the area.

This was not something I ever asked for; it was just something I had confirmed through many mature believers as witnesses. As I matured, I had many spiritual mothers and fathers that would help me in the process of discovering who I am in Christ and how I function in the Body. Discernment of spirits is just one of the many gifts that God has given me. One time I might be "a foot", another time "the mouth", another time "an ear." The point is that I know who I am in Him first, so that no matter where I am, I can just be in Him and open to what He wants ME to do in any given situation. 1 Corinthians 12:11 says, *"All these are empowered by one and the same Spirit, who apportions to each one individually as He wills."* I realized that it wasn't me at all but the Holy Spirit in me doing what He willed, because I had surrendered my will to His.

So for us to minister effectively, we must be willing to submit to the authority of another person, like our pastor or a mentor, so that they can help our character line up with the calling on our lives. It is not enough to have the gifts; we must know how and when to use them. If our character doesn't fit the timing of our release for ministry, we are setting ourselves up for a fall.

I used to complain that the one in authority over me was the one hindering me from moving forward. However, it was God using that person to prevent me from moving forward too soon, so that I wouldn't get wounded or killed in the process. In the armed forces, you must go through boot camp and training before you can be put on the battlefield. And even there you are put under layers of authority for protection. God's army is no different. I cannot teach a new Believer spiritual warfare without first making sure they have a solid foundation regarding how to use the weapons of warfare; otherwise, when they go out to battle they will be "killed," perhaps even literally. It is crucial to stay under authority at all times! It is in these very places that we will be tested to listen to God's ultimate authority. It is the place that rejection, ego and pride must be slain and surrendered to Christ.

2 Timothy 2:15, 21 says, "Do your best to present yourself to God as one approved, a worker who has no need to be ashamed, rightly handling the word of truth. Therefore, if anyone cleanses himself from what is dishonorable, he will be a vessel for honorable use, set apart as holy, useful to the master of the house, ready for every good work."

**Read and study these passages on the gifts of the Holy Spirit: 1 Corinthians 12:1-11, Romans 12:1-8, Ephesians 4:7-16**

1.    1 Corinthians 12:7 says <u>to each</u> is given the manifestation of the _____

2.    List the gifts you see in 1 Corinthians 12: 1-11

_____

_____

_____

_____

_____

_____

3.    We are to have _____ judgment about ourselves; by whom are these gifts given in accordance to our faith? (Romans 12:31) _____

4.    We will have gifts differ according to the _____ given to us. (Romans 12:6)

5.    What are some of the gifts listed in Romans 12:1-8?

_____

_____

_____

6.　According to Ephesians 4:7, who ascended and gave us these gifts?

_____

7.　What are the gifts listed in Ephesians 4:7-16?

_____

_____

_____

8.　What office gifts are listed? In Ephesians 4:11-13 what are they to be used for? (Note: only a few are called to these positions in the body of Christ)

_____

_____

_____

9.　According to Ephesians 4:15, who are we to grow up into?

_____

10.　What happens when each part is working properly? (Ephesians 4:16)

_____

_____

Did you notice that some of the same gifts are listed more than once in these three chapters? Even though some of the same gifts are listed, they function at different levels. All of us in The Body of Christ are called to function in the gifts listed in 1Corinthians 12 in our everyday life. These are to be used to equip and empower a local church and bring hope to those seeking Christ. The gifts listed in Romans 12 are ministry gifts. These are gifts that have been given to individuals to bring forth the ministry calling that has been placed on their lives. These are for ministries outside of the church, for a larger portion of the Body. While these gifts also help train and equip, they function on a regional or local level. The Ephesians 4 gifts are at the highest level of functioning. They are to equip those who serve at a national, or even international, level. These undergird a majority of people at one time to help a maximum number of Believers do what they are called to do.

We are all called to manifest His power through the gifts He has given to us. It is a gift of power from your Heavenly Father to equip you to do His will. Pray and seek God as to what your spiritual gifts might be. Ask the Lord to have someone more mature than you in Christ confirm these gifts. If you have never taken a spiritual inventory, this might be a good place to start.

Many good inventories can be found by doing a search on the internet, and many of them are free. Journal what you believe you hear the Lord saying to you. Be sure to get confirmation of these gifts from a mature Believer.

Let's pray

*Father, Thank You that when Jesus ascended, You sent Your Holy Spirit to come upon us and fill us with Your power. Father, you left us these gifts so we can have Your power here on earth and accomplish Your will. Lord, show me my gifts and how to use them. Enhance them for Your glory, that You will be known throughout the earth. I choose to hide in Your presence, so that others will not see me but You, moving through me. Help me to steward these gifts You have given me. You have entrusted them to me and I give them back to You to use for Your glory alone.*

**Bonding with the Father: Knowing His gifts and power**
❖ **Matthew 7:11**
❖ **Acts 1:8**
❖ **Romans 11:29**
❖ **Hebrews 2:4**

**Memorize:**

*"Truly, truly, I say to you, whoever believes in Me will also do the works that I do; and greater works than these will he do, because I am going to the Father. Whatever you ask in My name, this I will do, that the Father may be glorified in the Son. If you ask me anything in my name, I will do it. John 14:12-14*

# Lesson 30 - Knowing your Spheres of Authority

*"Enlarge the place of your tent, and let them stretch out the curtains of your dwellings. Do not spare, lengthen your cords, and strengthen your stakes. For you shall expand to the right and to the left. And your descendants will inherit the nations, and make the desolate cities inhabited."*
*Isaiah 54:2-3 (NKJV)*

In a previous lesson, I mentioned the different spheres of authority: self, family, church, community and region. As you grow in the Lord, He expands "the stakes of your tent"– your area of authority (Isaiah 54:2). It is imperative that you know your times and seasons before you venture out into new territory. Many of us get anxious when we have been given a word from God to do some task. We too often feel it is something that needs to be done "right now." But before we can embark on the task, we need to ask the Lord for His timing. The Lord first needs to give us words of direction to prepare our character to line up with our calling.

Look at Moses. As an heir to the throne of Pharaoh, he tried taking matters into his own hands before it was time. He ended up killing a man and being exiled into the wilderness. (Exodus 2:14) Once God had him in the wilderness for a season, he was prepared for the task of freeing God's people from slavery. If we don't allow the Lord to keep us in our place – if we fight to move forward too soon – we can bring trouble and pain to our selves and those around us. You may have a sense that you are to minister overseas, but if you are not properly prepared, you can get burned-out or hurt in the process. Some of us are called to minister solely within the local church. Some are called to minister in the city or region where they live. Others are called to minister within their state or nation. And others are called to minister internationally. The key is to allow the Lord to build you up where you are BEFORE you jump to the next level. You must be sensitive to the times and seasons of the Lord.

For a season, the Lord had me building a prayer ministry within our church. My passion was to build a prayer shield around our pastor. Later, I was asked to build a prayer ministry around a Christian camp and retreat center. From there, I was asked to build a statewide prayer shield around our state's prayer leaders serving a governmental alliance network.

The disciples were taught to know their place, where and to whom they were called to minister. Jesus taught them daily, in a deeply close relationship with them, before He sent them out. When He did send them out, after over a year and a half of discipleship, He sent them out in pairs, never alone. Only then were they able to put into practice what they had seen Jesus doing. It is very important that you have a mentor as well, who can disciple you in the area in which you are called. This help is crucial to your place of future ministry.

Currently, my husband and I are disciplining over a dozen people while making sure that we have different people speaking into our lives as well. The other crucial aspect of discipleship is making sure you maintain Pastoral Covering. My husband, as the head of our household, covers me, and we cover those to whom we minister. This builds layers of protection. Remember, we are not fighting flesh and blood, but the powers and principalities of darkness! "Plans are established by counsel; by wise guidance wage war." (Proverbs 20:18) God never designed The Body of Christ on earth to be full of "lone rangers"; we are designed to work together. "Iron sharpens iron, and one man sharpens another." (Proverbs 27:17)

I become very concerned when I ask someone what church they belong to and they say they don't belong to any given church; they say they attend and visit many churches and don't feel led to settle down in any one church. Some may even answer that God has told them not to belong to one church. I am sorry to say this, but that is not God! That is a lie from the enemy to keep you exposed to danger and not walking in the places where the Lord has called you. You must have a church membership and a pastoral covering to keep you effective in your spiritual battles.

Even if your calling is to visit and minister to other churches, you must still have that pastoral covering. You must have been sent out by your church membership, which hopefully, has laid hands on you and anointed you into your ministry. (Acts 6:3-6; Acts 13:1-3) The Lord has designed ministry to have protective covering. To not submit to someone, to a pastoral covering, is rebellion and must be corrected before effective ministry can take place. Mike and I will not mentor anyone who has not first submitted to their pastoral covering, and we always seek their pastor's permission to mentor them. When you have been faithful in the little things, the Father will trust you with even more!

## Read Matthew 10:1-16 & Matthew 8:5-13

1.   What did Jesus give the disciples authority to do?

_____

2.   Where did He tell them to go?

_____

_____

3.   What was their specific assignment?

_____

_____

4.   What was His warning in Matthew 10:16?

_____

_____

5.   What was the centurion asking Jesus to do?

_____

_____

6.   Why did he not want Jesus to come to his house (Matthew 8:8)?

_____

_____

## *The Outward Journey: Manifesting His Authority*

Take note in these passages from Matthew that Jesus <u>first</u> commissioned His disciples and <u>then</u> He sent them out under His authority. In the second passage, the centurion understood authority, the authority he walked in as well as the authority Jesus had to heal his servant without Jesus needing to be there. It was the centurion's faith in Jesus' authority that healed his servant.

We have been given the same authority Jesus gave the disciples. If we are not able to be obedient with the little authority He gives us He will not give us more. It is crucial to stay where He has us to grow, before we try to move out in authority we don't have. John 7:18 states, "The one who speaks on his own authority seeks his own glory, but the one who seeks the glory of him who sent him is true, and in him there is no falsehood." God has called us to be accountable to and discipled by those who are in authority. When we walk in God's designated authority, we walk in a greater measure of His anointing. When Joshua was fighting in battle, he knew he was under the covering of Moses; if Moses was lifting him up in prayer, then he would continue to win. It was his covering under Moses, who was under the Lord's covering, that gave Joshua the authority to conquer his enemies.

There have been times when I felt the urge to move forward in something and my husband and pastor told me the timing was not right. If I had stepped out, I would have been stepping out of the authority the Lord had set up for me. Jesus only spoke on the authority of the Father (John 12:49). How much more are we to submit to those He has in authority over us? (Romans 13:1) God is our ultimate authority. When we are properly aligned, we can flow in the freedom of His power and anointing.

Let's Pray

*Father, through the blood of Jesus I submit myself to You first and foremost. Grant me revelation of the authority You have allotted to me as Your child. Help me to grow in that authority and in obedience. May I never bring shame but only glory to You. Show me those to whom I am to submit. Forgive me for walking out in my own pride, outside of Your authority and the authority of others. Realign me with those You to whom you want me to submit and minister alongside.*

Write what you hear the Lord saying then begin to worship him for his answers

_____

_____

_____

_____

_____

_____

_____

_____

_____

_____

_____

_____

_____

_____

_____

_____

_____

_____

_____

_____

_____

_____

_____

**Bonding with the Father: Understanding His Authority**
- ❖  Matthew 9:6-8
- ❖  Matthew 28:18
- ❖  Luke 4:6
- ❖  John 10:18; 16:13
- ❖  2 Corinthians 13:10

**Memorize:**

*"And Jesus came and said to them, 'All authority in heaven and on earth has been given to me.'" Matthew 28:18*

Wow! It's hard to believe, but our Journey has ended! I've had a wonderful time taking this Journey with you. Let's just thank the Lord together for this journey.

*Heavenly Father, we thank You for transforming our hearts and bringing Your healing presence. May this journey never end but be a continual process of reaching upward, and allowing You deeper inward, so we can do more for You outward...Amen*

# More of God's Attributes:

Feel free to study these as you continue your journey.

He is our Sovereign (absolute in authority, in control) Lord: Psalm 103:19-22; Job 42:2; Psalm 135:6-7

He is our Friend: Exodus 33:11a; Proverbs 18:24; John 15:9-17

He is our Kinsman Redeemer: Job 19-25; Proverbs 23:11; Isaiah 44:6; Psalm 78:35

He is our Peace: Isaiah 26:3-4; John 14:2; Colossians 1:19-20

He is our Shepherd/Nurturer: Psalm 23; Isaiah 40:11; Ezekiel 24:11-23

He is our Provider: Genesis 22:8; 13-14; Acts 14:17; Philippians 4:19

He is our Comforter: Psalm 71:17-22; 94:17-19; Isaiah 66:13; 2 Corinthians 1:3-5

He is our Healer: Exodus15:22-26; Deuteronomy 32:39; Matthew 8:16-17

He is our Deliverer: 2 Samuel 22:17-20; Psalm 91; Ephesians 2:3-9

He is our Bread of Life: John 6:35-38; 48-51

He is our Living Water: John 4:10-15

He is our Guide/Counselor/Teacher: Psalm 119:24; Isaiah 9:6; Isaiah 28:29; John 14:16-17, 25-27; John 15:26, 16:7-15

# His Healing Love

*Scriptural prayers you can pray for yourself or others.*

❤   "You (insert name here) love righteousness and hate wickedness; Therefore God, your God, has anointed you with oil of gladness more than your companions. Listen, O daughter, Consider and incline your ear; Forget your people, and forget your father's house; So the King will greatly desire your beauty; Because He *is* your Lord, worship Him" Psalm 45:7, 10-11 (NKJV)

❤   "The Lord appeared to me from far away. I have loved you (insert name here) with an everlasting love; I have loved you with an everlasting love; therefore I have continued my faithfulness to you. Jeremiah 31:3

❤   "When (insert name here) was a child, I loved him, and out of Egypt (bondage) I called my son. Yet it was I who taught you how to walk, taking you by your arms; but you did not realize it was I who healed you. I led you with cords of human kindness, and with bands of love; I lifted the yoke from your necks and bent down to you and fed you." Hosea 11:1, 3-4

❤   "On the day you (insert name here) were born your cord was not cut, nor were you washed with water to cleanse you, nor rubbed with salt, nor wrapped in swaddling cloths. No eye pitied you, to do any of these things to you out of compassion for you, but you were cast out on the open field, for you were abhorred. AND WHEN I passed by you and saw you wallowing in your blood, I said to you in your blood, 'LIVE!'

I said to you in your blood "LIVE!' I made you flourish like a plant of the field. And you grew up and became tall and arrived at full adornment. Your breasts were formed, and your hair had grown; yet you were naked and bare. When I passed by you again and saw you, behold, you were at the age for love, and I spread the corner of my garment over you and covered your nakedness; I made my vow to you and entered into a covenant with you, declares the Lord God, and you became Mine. Then I bathed you with water and washed off your blood from you and anointed you with oil. I clothed you also with embroidered cloth and shod you with fine leather. I wrapped you in fine linen and covered you with silk. And I adorned you with ornaments and put bracelets on your wrists and a chain on your neck. And I put a ring on your nose and earrings in your ears and a beautiful crown on your head. Thus you were adorned with gold and silver, and your clothing was of fine linen and silk and embroidered cloth. You ate fine flour and honey and oil. You grew exceedingly beautiful and advanced to royalty. And your renown went forth among the nations because of your beauty, for it was perfect through the splendor that I had bestowed on you, declares the Lord God." Ezekiel 16:4-14

❤  "He brought me to His banqueting house and His banner over me is love." Song of Solomon 2:4

❤  "For you formed (insert name here) inward parts; You knitted me together in my mother's womb. I praise You, for I am fearfully and wonderfully made. Wonderful are your works; (since I am your works, I am wonderful) my soul knows it very well. My frame was not hidden from You when I was being made in secret, intricately woven in the depths of the earth. Your eyes saw my unformed substance; in Your book were written, every one of them, the days that were formed for me, when as yet there was none of them. How precious to me are Your thoughts, O God! How vast is the sum of them!" Psalm 139:13-17

❤  "For I know the plans I have for you (insert name here), declares the Lord, plans for welfare and not for evil, to give you a future and a hope. Then you will call upon me and come and pray to me, and I will hear you. You will seek me and find me when you seek me with all your heart. I will be found by you, declares the Lord, and I will restore your fortunes and gather you from all the nation and places where I have driven you." Jeremiah 29:11-14a

❤  "I will give you (insert name here) the treasures of darkness and hoards in secret places, that you may know that it is I, the Lord the God of Israel, who called you by your name. I call you by your name, I name you, though you do not know me." Isaiah 45:3-4

❤  "My beloved speaks and says to me, "Arise, my love, my beautiful one, and come away, for behold, the winter is past; the rain is over and gone. The flowers appear on the earth, the time of the singing [of birds] has come, and the voice of the turtledove is heard in our land. The fig tree ripens its figs, and the vines are in blossom; they give forth fragrance. Arise, my love, my beautiful one, and come away. [So] I went with him, and when we were climbing the rocky steps up the hillside, my beloved shepherd said to [me], 'O my dove, [while you are here] in the clefts of the rock, in the crannies of the cliff, let me see your face, let me hear your voice; for your voice is sweet, and your face is lovely.'" Song of Solomon 2:10-14

## More...
- Psalm 45
- Song of Solomon chapters 2-4
- Isaiah 60:1-5
- Psalm 91
- Isaiah 40:28-31
- Ephesians 3:16-21
- Zephaniah 3:17
- Isaiah 58:11
- Psalm 116:15-19
- Hosea 2:19-20
- Jeremiah 30:17

# In Christ

In Christ I am justified
Romans 3:24

In Christ I am dead to sin
Romans 6:11

In Christ I have Eternal Life
Romans 6:23

In Christ, there is no condemnation for me
Romans 8:1

In Christ I am free from the law of sin
Romans 8:2

In Christ I have wisdom, justification, sanctification and
redemption
1 Corinthians 1:30

In Christ I am made alive
1 Corinthians 15:22

In Christ I am triumphant
2 Corinthians 2:14

In Christ I am a new creature
2 Corinthians 5:17

In Christ I am reconciled with God
2 Corinthians 5:19

In Christ, the blessing of Abraham is for me
Galatians 3:14

In Christ I am blessed by God
Ephesians 1:3

In Christ I am workmanship of God
Ephesians 2:10

In Christ I am made close to God
Ephesians 2:13

In Christ I am forgiven
Ephesians 4:32

Contact information:

April would love to hear from you! If this book has blessed you or helped you in anyway, please feel free to contact April at info@lscen.org

# End Notes:

### Chapter 1

[1] Lesson I - W.E. Vine, *Vines Concise Dictionary,* (Nashville, TN, Thomas Nelson, 1999), pg. 421

[2] Lesson 3 - W.E. Vine, *Vines Concise Dictionary,* (Nashville, TN, Thomas Nelson, 1999),

### Chapter 2

[1] Lesson 4 - W.E. Vine, *Vines Concise Dictionary,* (Nashville, TN, Thomas Nelson, 1999)

[2] Lesson 5 - W.E. Vine, *Vines Concise Dictionary,* (Nashville, TN, Thomas Nelson, 1999)

[3] Lesson 6 - W.E. Vine, *Vines Concise Dictionary,* (Nashville, TN, Thomas Nelson, 1999)

### Chapter 3

[1] Lesson 8 - W.E. Vine, *Vines Concise Dictionary,* (Nashville, TN, Thomas Nelson, 1999)

[2] Lesson 8 - W.E. Vine, *Vines Concise Dictionary,* (Nashville, TN, Thomas Nelson, 1999)

[3] Lesson 9 - Strong's Greek and Hebrew Concordance

### Chapter 4

[1] Lesson 10 - Thayer's Definition a Related Word by Thayer's/Strong's Number: from G3129

Citing in TDNT: 4:415, 552

[2] Lesson 10 - Thayer Definition: A Related Word by Thayer's/Strong's Number: a prolonged form of a primary verb G1097 Citing in TDNT: 1:689, 119

[3] Lesson 12 - Purification - consecration meaning a year of preparation for girls of the harem; bodily rubbings
From H4838; properly a *scouring*, that is, *soap* or *perfumery* for the bath; figuratively a *detergent:* - X cleanse, (thing for) purification - Strong's Greek and Hebrew Concordance

## Chapter 5
[1] Lesson 13 - Merriam-Webster Online Dictionary copyright © 2005 by Merriam-Webster, Incorporated
[2] Lesson 16 - Merriam-Webster Online Dictionary copyright © 2005 by Merriam-Webster, Incorporated
[3] Lesson 16 - A Related Word by Thayer's/Strong's Number: from a primary sos (contraction for obsolete saoz, "safe") Citing in TDNT: 7:965, 1132 1a1) to save a suffering one (from perishing), i.e. one suffering from disease, to make well, heal, restore to health

## Chapter 7
[1] Lesson 21- Strong's Greek and Hebrew Concordance

## Chapter 8
[1] Lesson 22- Strong's Greek and Hebrew Concordance
[1] Lesson 23 - Merriam-Webster Online Dictionary copyright © 2005 by Merriam-Webster, Incorporated

## Chapter 9
[1] Lesson 26 - Merriam-Webster Online Dictionary copyright © 2005 by Merriam-Webster, Incorporated
[1] Lesson 27 - Merriam-Webster Online Dictionary copyright © 2005 by Merriam-Webster, Incorporated

[2] Lesson 27 - C.S. Lewis Quote http://www.goodreads.com/quotes/201236-true- humility-is-not-thinking-less-of-yourself-it-is

**Chapter 10**

[1] Lesson 28 - Merriam-Webster Online Dictionary copyright © 2005 by Merriam-Webster, Incorporated

[2] Lesson 28 - http://www.religioustolerance.org/chr_dira.htm

[3] Lesson 28 - Jack Lambert story http://www.smorgasburgh.com/the-10-most-devastating-injuries-in-steelers-history/

Made in the USA
Middletown, DE
03 September 2023

37897091R00166